The Future of the European Past

T0149926

THE FUTURE
of the
EUROPEAN
PAST

EDITED WITH AN INTRODUCTION BY

Hilton Kramer

AND

Roger Kimball

IVAN R. DEE

Chicago 1997

The paperback edition of this book carries the following ISBN: 1-56663-581-0

THE FUTURE OF THE EUROPEAN PAST. Copyright © 1997
by Hilton Kramer and Roger Kimball. All rights reserved, including the right to
reproduce this book or portions thereof in any form. For information, address:
Ivan R. Dee, Inc., 1332 North Halsted Street, Chicago 60622. Manufactured in
the United States of America and printed on acid-free paper.

Library of Congress Cataloging-in-Publication Data:
The future of the European past / edited by Hilton Kramer and Roger Kimball.
    p. cm.
A collection of essays first published in "The new criterion."
Includes index.
    Contents: Introduction — Ancient ghosts stir / by David Pryce-Jones — A
dearth of feeling / by Anne Applebaum — The eclipse of listening / by Roger
Scruton — Knocking about the ruins / by John Gross — A devitalized wariness /
by Ferdinand Mount — Possessing the golden key / by John Herington — The
real stuff of history / by Keith Windschuttle — Present-tense culture / by Mark
Steyn — The postmodern assault / by Hilton Kramer — Experiments against
reality / by Roger Kimball
    ISBN 1-56663-178-5 (alk. paper)
    1. Europe—Civilization. 2. Europe—Politics and government. 3. United
States—Civilization—European influences. I. Kramer, Hilton. II. Kimball,
Roger, 1953–
D1055.F88 1997
940—dc21   97-26863

The editors dedicate this book
to the memory of

John Herington

ille deum vitam accipiet divisque videbit
permixtos heroas et ipse videbitur illis

Contents

Introduction

Writing in 1790, Edmund Burke reflected sadly on the likely consequences of the French Revolution and its wide-ranging attack on the legacy of the European past. Although the Terror was still more than two years off, Burke already saw the abyss into which the Revolution threatened to precipitate the accumulated cultural, moral, and political achievements that together made up what he called "the glory of Europe." "When antient opinions and rules of life are taken away," Burke wrote, "the loss cannot possibly be estimated. From that moment we have no compass to govern us; nor can we know distinctly to what port we steer."

> Now all is to be changed. . . . All the decent drapery of life is to be rudely torn off. All the super-added ideas, furnished from the wardrobe of a moral imagination, which the heart owns, and the understanding ratifies, as necessary to cover the defects of our naked shivering nature, and to raise it to dignity in our own estimation, are to be exploded as a ridiculous, absurd, and antiquated fashion.

Against the ruthless innovations of unanchored novelty, Burke commended the deliberate resources of the European past: a check to unseemly haste, a prop for irremediable incapacity, a guide and tutor for stubborn passions. "Tradition" is one word for this moral repository; "prejudice" was the word that Burke tended to favor. To modern ears, perhaps nothing in Burke sounds stranger than his praise of prejudice; for us, prejudice means enmity unschooled by reason. But for Burke, prejudice had a positive charge. It signified above all the distilled spontaneity of tradition. "Prejudices" were those "pre-judgments" that helped to "render a man's virtue his habit" by educating the pulse of feeling, civilizing manners, instinct, taste, and sensibility. As Burke understood, at issue was not so much the direction of reason as cultivation of the reasons of the heart, without which, he warned, we are condemned to the anarchy of moral weightlessness.

As we approach the year 2000 and a new millennium, Burke's premonitions gain a new urgency. The dazzling accomplishments of Western science and modern capitalism have made us vastly richer and technologically more competent than any society in history, while the institutions of liberal democracy have secured us an unparalleled degree of personal and political liberty. At the same time, however, the moral and cultural achievements of European civilization—the very achievements that underwrite our prosperity and give meaning and purpose to our liberty—are everywhere under attack.

In *Notes towards a Definition of Culture*, T. S. Eliot remarked that "culture may . . . be described simply as that which makes life worth living." The disturbing truth is that the vital commitments and (in Burke's sense) "prejudices" that nourish and perpetuate culture are in a state of advanced decay. In virtually every precinct of cultural life, latitudinarian political imperatives, abetted by the dead weight of historical ignorance, have worked like a corrosive acid, distorting and disfiguring the legacy of our European past. In American colleges and universities, the European past from the time of the Greeks on down is under indictment on charges of racism, sexism, and sundry other violations of politically correct standards of social policy. Institutions that once served as proud custodians of European cultural traditions—art museums, theaters, opera houses, ballet companies—have similarly come under fire for failing to meet the new political standards, and have hastened to alter their programs and productions accordingly. In the offices of every publication that engages in intellectual pursuits—from mass-circulation newspapers and magazines to small-circulation critical reviews and academic journals—the discussion of the European past has likewise become, in effect, a battleground for mapping out the future of our own culture.

The very concept of a liberal arts education is, of course, an invention of the European past. So is the idea of liberal democracy. This is why our universities and arts institutions have historically regarded themselves as the intellectual guardians of the Western tradition. Yet in the face of a concerted political assault from radical multiculturalists, on the one hand, and left-wing historical revisionists, on the other, the traditional priority given to the European past in American cultural life has been made an issue of fierce and contentious debate—not only in the classroom, the museums, and on the stages of our performing arts institutions, but in the halls of our legislatures and even in our courts of law. What is being demanded in the name of political correctness is nothing less than a sweeping repeal of our own cultural past insofar as it is seen to have been unduly "Eurocentric"—a term that has been transformed from a badge of honor into an accusatorial epithet.

In Europe, meanwhile, political and cultural developments raise many questions about the ability of our European contemporaries to deal with a debilitating crisis of confidence in regard to their own most exalted traditions. Immigration from the Third World, the war in Bosnia, and the spread of religious fanaticism have made the authority of Europe's cultural traditions problematic to Europe itself. So has the widespread embrace of the most debased varieties of American popular culture. The collapse of Communism in Eastern Europe and the loss of faith in the welfare state in at least some parts of Western Europe have created great opportunities for a renewal of Europe. And yet, as David Pryce-Jones argues in his essay "Ancient Ghosts Stir," the very concept of a centralized European "community" now threatens Europe with a form of bureaucratic collectivism that bears some dismaying resemblances to the totalitarian systems that have made so much of Europe's history in this century a nightmare.

With Islamic fundamentalism advancing from the East, a supra-welfare bureaucracy emerging from Brussels, a decadent popular culture everywhere annihilating custom, morals, and tradition, and newly inflamed ancient ethnic hatreds attempting to fill every spiritual void, it is not at all clear how much longer even Europe can hope to remain "Eurocentric" in its fundamental cultural loyalties.

It was in the hope of clarifying the prospects for European culture—*our* culture—as we approach the millennium that *The New Criterion* undertook this series of ten essays on the future of the European past. Our goal was primarily one of cultural diagnosis: What are the symptoms of our current crisis? What attitudes and policies have encouraged its development? What resources do we command to address it? The result is not a systematic analysis but a group of snapshots taken from various angles. Some of the essays deal with the fate of particular disciplines or art forms—classical music, the study of the Greek and Roman classics, art history—others deal more broadly with cultural-political trends in various segments of American and European society. As with any such collaborative portrait, readers will discover important differences of emphasis, perspective, and opinion among the contributions to this volume. But although there is no unanimity of opinion in these essays, there are some recurrent themes and concerns.

One recurrent theme is the ubiquity and destructive influence of pop culture. As John Gross observes in "Knocking about the Ruins,"

> Many of the ingredients of the common brew will be tediously familiar to Americans; most of them, indeed, are American in origin. Rock, rap, Rollerblades; Disney and McDonald's; Quentin Tarantino, Beavis and Butt-head, Michael Jackson; and, if you want a handy symbol to sum up the whole phenomenon, you couldn't do much better, for the moment, than the ubiquitous baseball cap. . . .
>
> There is, of course, nothing new about the enormous impact of American popular culture in Europe. It is a story as old as Hollywood and Tin Pan Alley; as old as Phineas T. Barnum (and in some respects, let it be said, a tribute to the superior energy and efficiency of the American product). But two things have changed over the past generation or so. First, Europeans have become more adept at generating mass entertainment and catering for mass consumption, in a manner which may still ultimately derive from American models but is far from merely imitative. (The Beatles were an obvious landmark here.) Secondly,

pop culture is now so pervasive that it is thought of as being international rather than primarily American. There is much less transatlantic glamour attaching to it than there once was. It is part of the air that everybody breathes.

The inescapability of popular culture is one problem. Its increasing perniciousness is another. Anyone concerned about the future of the European past must view the accelerating degradation and viciousness of even mainstream popular culture with alarm. The widespread "dumbing down" of pop culture and its glorification of violence, sexual pathology, and hedonistic consumerism are disturbing symptoms of a culture that has gone dangerously astray.

The problem is not simply the everyday life of pop culture—bad though that is. In some ways even more worrisome is the acceptance, indeed the celebration, of pop culture—even in its most mindless and corrupting manifestations—by intellectuals. Already in the 1950s, the political philosopher Hannah Arendt noted in "The Crisis in Culture" that the chief danger to society came not from the purveyors of popular culture but from

> a special kind of intellectual, often well read and well informed, whose sole function is to organize, disseminate, and change cultural objects in order to persuade the masses that *Hamlet* can be as entertaining as *My Fair Lady*, and perhaps educational as well. There are many great authors of the past who have survived centuries of oblivion and neglect, but it is still an open question whether they will be able to survive an entertaining version of what they have to say.

Arendt wrote at a time when this process was only beginning to make itself felt. Today the "special kind of intellectual" she describes has become the norm, bent not only on transforming all culture into a form of entertainment but also on erasing the very distinction between high culture and entertainment. These are points upon which Mark Steyn reflects in his essay "Present-Tense Culture."

> It's not that pop stars want to be intellectuals, but that intellectuals want to be pop stars—a uniquely contemporary crisis. The threat to the European past comes not from mass vulgarization but from elite vulgarization. The most popular forms of contemporary culture—"Dr. Quinn, Medicine Woman," *The Bridges of Madison County*, Whitney Houston and Céline Dion ballads—are unchanged in their bourgeois sentimental efficiency from their equivalents a hundred years ago. What's different is that, whereas a century ago our betters were telling us to put down our parlor ballads for Mozart and Beethoven, now they tell us we should be listening to Rapeman or Suicide.

Everywhere one turns, distinctions are erased: between high and low, accomplished and mediocre, better and worse, proper and improper. It's not simply that rap lyrics are elevated in status to the point where they are now studied in colleges alongside Shakespeare (absurd and destructive though that development admittedly is): no, even as rap music is elevated, Shakespeare is downgraded by the imperatives of social history. Shakespeare, too, must be regarded as another cultural "text," not essentially different from—and certainly not essentially better than—a rap lyric.

One might describe this process as the universalization of the democratic impulse: applying democratic imperatives to the cultural realm as well as to the political realm.

In fact, though, it is not so much the universalization of democracy we are witnessing as its trivialization. Cultural egalitarianism transforms equality into the enemy instead of the companion of excellence. As the French philosopher Alain Finkielkraut noted in his book *La Défaite de la pensée* ("The Undoing of Thought"),

> The artist used to be at war with the Philistine. Today, for fear of being tainted with élitism or with failing to meet the elementary requirements of the democratic outlook, your intellectual abases himself before the power-hungry world of show-business, or fashion, or advertising. The extraordinarily rapid transformation of ministers of cultural affairs into administrators concerned with entertainment as such, passes without comment.

In other words, what we have witnessed is an epidemic of intellectual slumming: a failure of principle that is at the same time a corruption of sensibility. The pseudo-Dionysian appeal of rock music—and the drug culture that accompanied its rapid triumph throughout the world—has played an important and still incompletely appreciated role in this cultural *dégringolade*, helping to legitimize novel forms of hedonistic abandon and undermining salutary habits of restraint and emotional delicacy.

The future of the European past is threatened in other ways as well. A second recurring theme in these essays concerns the prospects of traditional humanistic inquiry and the study of languages it presupposes. In "Possessing the Golden Key," the classicist John Herington argues that

> in the last resort it is language that lies nearest to the heart, whatever society, whatever literature is under study. The

future integrity of classical studies, if not their survival, depends ultimately on the future of Greek and Latin learning. Only if such learning continues can we look forward to genuine, firsthand research, or count on the honesty of future translations. Much the same, of course, will apply to the study of any of the other great national literatures that have arisen on the European continent; the future of the European past generally seems to be bound up with the future of language studies.

As anyone familiar with the state of academic research in the humanities today knows, we are faced with an increasingly grave crisis of literacy. Indeed, the crisis is twofold. Not only is there a widespread failure of literacy on the rudimentary level—more and more people are simply unable to read and write competently—but also there is a corruption of language at the highest levels that amounts to a new form of elite illiteracy. Answering to the brute illiteracy of the masses is the polysyllabic illiteracy of the overeducated. Aggravating both sorts of illiteracy are the host of seductive technological innovations that, notwithstanding their undeniable power as tools of communication, threaten to undermine literacy even further by undermining the primacy of our commitment to language and literature. "Anyone who sets out to predict any aspect of future society," Mr. Herington points out,

> must begin by acknowledging that we are now in the midst of a cultural transition compared to which the transitions from oral to written literature, and from manuscript to print, may prove to have been quite minor affairs. When the elementary schools are being wired for the Internet, who knows what is about to happen, for good or

ill, to the entire educational and social structure? Is the book likely to preserve its primacy, or even, in the long run, its existence as an instrument of education or entertainment? Will the *word* (whether spoken or printed or just looming greenly on a computer screen) be able to make headway against the roaring torrent of visual images?

The essays in this volume (several of which have been revised and expanded since they first appeared in *The New Criterion*) cover a great many topics, from the fall of Communism in Eastern Europe to the corruption of historical studies under the influence of cultural studies, deconstruction, and other efforts to blur the distinction between historical fact and fiction. If there is an element common to them all, it is a concern with what Burke might have called the rehabilitation of prejudice: the rehabilitation of those unspoken commitments and modes of feeling that link us with the past, not as something dead and behind us, but as the surest source of strength for what lies ahead.

HK
RK
July 1997

The Future of the European Past

Ancient Ghosts Stir

David Pryce-Jones

B ORN in Vienna, caught in France by the war, I am old
enough to remember escaping from the Germans, the
sensation of hunger, and the shudder of bombs. A soldier
myself in due course, I was stationed with the British army
near Düsseldorf, in the Rhineland. At the time, shop-
keepers in the mighty Königsallee running through that
city used to operate from smashed piles of rubble, their
stock of goods on a single tray. Today the Königsallee is
a consumer's mecca, and as expensive as real estate any-
where. Much was obliterated or looted in the war, but
governments and the whole range of developers have since
carried the process further. Hardened old Europe, as Henry
James called it, could evidently absorb an awful lot of
ruin.

The softened new Europe is not without merit. Nobody
starves. Bombs drop only in faraway countries of which
we know nothing, like Bosnia. Germans have acquired a
democratic outlook. Cities sprout steel girders and plate
glass as their commercial districts and industrial zones extend along ring-roads and bypasses toward housing estates,
urban sprawl, and finally suburbs. The external glow of
prosperity is unmistakable. But a cluster of related political
concepts, and their social and moral consequences, conspire
to reduce that prosperity to an end in itself. Poverty of spirit

is the price to be paid. And absence of culture is not synonymous with well-being.

Definitions of culture, according to the century's most famous poet, do not go beyond notes. Yet everyone has a sense of the thing. Popular culture was the sharing of activities and experience with one's fellows, and also the pointer to the questions of higher culture: what was the nature of fulfillment and completion, and how were human beings to reconcile themselves to this world and the next? Choice and choosing were at the heart of the answer. Worth in an individual was to be judged by the choices he made, and the manner of his choosing. Art had the purpose of showing how choices came to be taken, and how fraught choosing is. Tragedy and comedy elide into one another unforeseeably. Description is the key to the shifts of reality. Differentiated by language, law, and religion, European nation-states had their own particular identities and cultures. But the more closely the artist could show what were the consequences of action, the greater his claim to universality.

The word culture has narrowed its meaning to the point where sentences such as these sound remote. Culture has come to mean some sort of group behavior or gratification, a special interest rather than the expression of a complete personality. Rock culture. Football culture. "The culture of barbarity," said someone interviewed on television about Northern Ireland, while someone else advocated "the culture of civility." Or the Archbishop of Canterbury: "One of society's greatest difficulties is the cultural tendency to regard morality as no more than a matter of individual opinion." True no doubt, but he was confusing culture with ethics. Copenhagen, it appears, is this year's cultural capital of the European Union. In practice, this turned out to be the staging of a Euro-pride festival, with workshops and exhibitions, and then a parade of thirty thousand homosexuals. The gay culture within the arts and crafts culture, and both within the would-be Euro-culture.

How did higher culture lose its vitality and purpose, coming to rest in the hands of university departments, to be analyzed rather than lived? How did popular culture come to be a range of leisure activities? Matthew Arnold, Julien Benda, Ortega y Gasset, and many more had warned that this might happen; some of them prophetically, others with a touch of neurosis or charlatanry. Things would probably have gone on as before, had it not been for the destructive but historically definitive series of events that led to Nazism and Communism.

For true believers in these comparable ideologies, the individual's fulfillment and completion lay in submission to the collective to which he happened to belong through the unalterable fact of birth into a particular class or race. In human matters down to inessential details, choices were predetermined for him. Traditional culture was incompatible, and Nazis and Communists alike were determined to do away with it. In practice, the universal component of both proved to be standardization through force. Wherever Nazism or Communism held sway, a facsimile of culture was deliberately manufactured, with mass rallies and shows of military strength, gymnastics and folk dancing, and all things mindless. Forbidden to reflect choice, literature and art became aspects of ideology.

The poems of Mayakovsky, the Palaces of Culture and Stalinist wedding-cake architecture, Khachaturian jingles and firing-squad prose in the Sholokhov mode were of a piece with the Haus der Kunst, the sculptures of Arno Breker and the models of Albert Speer, the vaporings of

Stefan George and Martin Heidegger, the martial tempo of SS Colonel Herbert von Karajan. But in the other scale of the balance was mass murder as a social good.

In one of his essays, Elie Kedourie tells the story of an unknown inhabitant of Baghdad who over a century ago recorded in his diary the tyranny of the ruler of his day. To have witnessed such violence, Kedourie wrote, was itself "a kind of bruised and forlorn glory." However brutal that moment, it was nothing compared to the Europe of the dictators. In the manner of that anonymous inhabitant of Baghdad, there were some who bore witness: Primo Levi, Paul Celan, Tadeusz Borowski, Varlam Shalamov, Mikhail Bulgakov, Solzhenitsyn. More than a forlorn glory, theirs was an envoi. As in the parable of Adam and Eve, there is no going back to innocence.

Accidental or personal as it may seem, choice involves moral discrimination between right and wrong. Nazism and Communism simplified every course of action. You resisted or you collaborated. Bystanders and good Samaritans had no role. Collaborating with these ideologies, the majority of European intellectuals surrendered the capacity to choose of their own free will. An elite that so easily lost its moral authority inspires mistrust.

Nowhere has this been so dire as in France. French literature and painting had set standards against which artists everywhere measured themselves. France, birthplace of the rights of man, was unable to stand up to Hitler's Germany. There seems to have been a failure at every level, psychological and physical and political. Jean-Baptiste Duroselle gave his account of the Thirties in France the bald title *La Décadence*. André Gide was perhaps the foremost French writer of the period. He had seen through the Soviet Union and its deceptions. On the day that the

German army marched into Paris without a shot fired, he wrote in his diary that events had revealed the country's profound decay. Soon afterwards, he had a gloss: "To come to terms with yesterday's enemy is not cowardice but wisdom; as well as accepting what is inevitable." But Nazi victory was inevitable only if the people chose to let it be so.

When Marshal Pétain and Pierre Laval and their colleagues announced their collaboration with Hitler, unquestionably almost everyone in France was relieved. The record shows how readily French intellectuals accepted the opportunities and careers opened to them in the France of a military governor, of Otto Abetz, the German ambassador, and Dr. Karl Epting of the German Institute. Abetz is credited with the crack that the powerhouses of Europe were the Vatican, the Communist Party, the Prussian general staff, and the *Nouvelle Revue française*. With its chaste white cover and red and black lettering, the NRF fell into line along with everyone else. Gerhard Heller, an official of Goebbels's Ministry of Propaganda, was the censor who placed the swastika stamp of approval on books and plays and journals. His is the autobiography of a man proud to have been accepted at the center of Parisian intellectual life.

A few like Albert Camus, François Mauriac, and André Malraux actively resisted in their ways. Jean-Paul Sartre was only one among many who claimed to resist but actually presented his work to be stamped with the swastika. Another famous German to spend the war in Paris was the novelist Ernst Jünger, whose diaries describe social life much as it had been prewar. He visited Picasso's studio, where German officers were keen buyers. You and I, Picasso observed one day to Jünger, could resolve the war in twenty-four hours.

Some sort of moral reckoning did occur. Laval was one of seven hundred executed for treason. The *épuration*, or purge, was haphazard and vindictive. As early as 1953, frightened authorities decreed an amnesty. Collaboration is a subject so hedged in with legal restrictions that it cannot be written about with honesty, and therefore festers.

In the Nazi wake came the Soviet occupation of Eastern Europe, fronted by local Communists or their colleagues or masters who had spent the war in Moscow. The archives have not yet revealed exactly what Stalin's intentions were as he toyed with extending into France and Italy, possibly elsewhere, too, the series of coups that secured Eastern Europe. Party activists in France and Italy, until lately armed partisans and *franc-tireurs*, expected to seize power and were never to recover from disappointment that they were not permitted to do so. The slow grind was instead put into motion to convince electorates to vote for the Party. The archives do reveal Moscow's comprehensive purpose and the gigantic sums of money expended on it: tens of millions of dollars in France and Italy, and the placing of thousands of agents of influence, especially in Germany. A British Communist has described how he used to pick up an annual suitcase with a million pounds in cash from the Soviet Embassy. Speeches of Communist deputies in the French National Assembly were drafted for them in Moscow. Those who had ruled France for Hitler had not sunk so low in obeisance.

Prewar fellow traveling had been a personal affair, a self-deception arising from character, often with misplaced idealism. Postwar collaboration was its extension into a mass movement of opinion. For almost half a century, a pro-Soviet climate bloomed in the face of all evidence about the true face of the Soviet regime. Hardly had the German officers left his studio than Picasso was drawing his "peace" symbols on behalf of the Soviet Union and publicly proclaiming that "one goes to the Communist Party as to a spring of fresh water." Countless lesser men and women shared the agility of his careerism. Any element of idealism was soon lost in venality.

By means of the Moscow subsidies, local Communist parties built up impressive patronage networks. In addition to their own declared outlets, they controlled or influenced newspapers, radio, and then television channels; they packed committees with power to promote Party writers and artists, set up front organizations, festivals, summer camps, and youth movements; ensured that Marxist courses were taught in schools and universities, and infiltrated even religious bodies. The Soviet future seemed a fact of life.

Alleged to be "bourgeois," cultural and moral standards were attacked unremittingly. Largely worthless writers and artists became household names: natural-born commissars like Louis Aragon and Maurice Merleau-Ponty, Genet, Althusser, Pasolini and many an Italian film-maker, Renato Guttoso and many a painter, and of course Bertolt Brecht, whose style of Party propaganda spread from East Berlin to become the prototype of contemporary theater. Never mind the earlier swastika stamps, Sartre justified the Soviet cause throughout the Cold War. Soviet wrong-doing could not exist, he argued, and if it did then it was a duty to hide it. He went so far as to deny the existence of gulag. Vicious controversies engulfed George Orwell, Arthur Koestler, Raymond Aron, Karl Popper, and anyone else who criticized the new climate of opinion as once they had criticized Nazism.

Fortunately the Soviet world folded up without the loss of life and physical damage of the war against Nazism. Reputations have evaporated along with the subsidies. The Sartres and Brechts and their imitators look like creatures of long-spent fashion, the equivalent of flappers in cloche hats. But this time there has been no moral reckoning. To date, only François Furet in his book *Le Passé d'une illusion* has attempted any systematic account of how such a range of intelligent people let themselves be duped into betraying fundamental human values. Conceding that former Communists like himself were wrong all along the line, he nevertheless tries to argue that in the context they could not have acted otherwise—a banal cancellation of his own apologia.

Freed from the external onslaught of collective ideology, it might be supposed, the human being and his fate could again become the cultural preoccupations that they once were, at the center of literary narrative and artistic representation. But all the while a secondary process of collectivism was undermining any such outcome.

Each country in Europe is now a democracy, and every one of them is also a modern welfare state offering its citizens rights at least to housing, education, and healthcare, "from cradle to grave." The origins of the welfare state are mixed. Philanthropists sincerely wished to improve the general lot by abolishing long-lasting inequities and injustices. Bismarck believed that this was the way to have better soldiers. Voted into power, the social democratic wing of Marxism saw it as a vehicle for the slogan "to each according to his needs." But only the Cold War brought about its full realization. In the deeper intentions of those who introduced it, the welfare state would pre-empt revolution in general, and the Soviet Union in particular.

When the British welfare state came into existence, its architect, William Beveridge, wrote to the then prime minister, Clement Attlee. He was proud to survey his handiwork, he declared, but went on to wonder whether he might not have subverted the British character. In theory, people were to have more choices to do with their lives what they wanted and so to fulfill themselves. But were politicians not tampering with the values that gave the individual his worth? Hitherto, people had been obliged to take responsibility for themselves; now the state would shoulder that responsibility.

People once used to think long and hard about breaking up their families, having an abortion, bearing children out of wedlock, committing criminal or antisocial acts. Responsibility for oneself entailed the punishment and shame of wrong choices, the recognition and approval of right choices.

By means of the welfare state and its many and various agencies, choices that determine the lives of others have been widely handed to officials and bureaucrats, the panoply of inspectors, social workers, therapists, consultants, managers, and not least politicians exchanging benefits for votes. That part of the population sustained by the welfare state forms the dependency culture, as powerful as it is immobilizing. As Beveridge suspected, actions cease to have consequences. Instead of right and wrong choices to be rewarded or punished, there are only cases to be dealt with.

Everywhere, of course, there are intellectuals and artists capable of contributing to the high culture they inherited. Quite unwittingly, the democratic welfare state is the main factor that inhibits such contribution, stifling what it aspires to foster. The array of Beaux Arts, English Heritage, and other preservation lobbies, the Arts Councils and Ministries of Culture, either take the past out of circulation and place it in pickling jars, or sponsor a uniform present, touristified, or more often than not, "experimental." In Venice, the Assessore per la Cultura spoke for all this kind. "The town is packed with dynamic academics who are reconsidering all the ways in which this deeply traditional city functions," and he went on: "Instead of just consuming—wearing out—the art of the past, we need to add new cultural experiences, we need to use culture as a strategic variable in the reorganization and development of the town."

On May 9, alleged to be Europe Day, the French government staged a thousand musical events. In Britain there are five hundred and fifty arts festivals yearly, and in June alone there were twenty-three hundred officially sponsored musical events. Government funding on the one hand underwrites low culture, and on the other favors those who can manipulate the bureaucracy into patronizing someone or something they think chic. From both directions, high culture is shut out by institutions, including universities and publishing houses and the media, that otherwise would be supportive.

Comedy treats of manners, but there can be no manners unless they are widely shared and codified. Tragedy treats of choices mistakenly made for genuine reasons. Art that deals with "cases" devalues comedy and tragedy to a point of meaninglessness. When everything is relative, any one course of action is as valid as another. And a case is merely a lifestyle. Young authors in Britain, Salman Rushdie pointed out, can talk about nothing except contemporary English lifestyles. Is there a European artist or writer born since 1945 for whom universality is an aim? Junking liturgy, bowdlerizing the Bible and prayer book into populist and sometimes ungrammatical lingo, the Catholic and Protestant churches have transformed even religion into an alternative lifestyle. In Germany, "churches have organised rave parties for the young," in the words of a recent article, and have held markets and mounted theatrical productions in them, "including a play with a topless actress and Christ with a gas-mask."

Brutalism, structuralism, deconstruction, postmodernism, minimalism, the Nouveau Roman, the *théâtre sans texte*, magical realism, and the rest of it, testify to the effort to thrash a way out of the predicament by discovering some sort of art as free from the whole business of choice as society itself is. This spreads the disease for which a cure is sought. The novel, the poem, the picture, history, morality itself, degrade into the entertainment business.

I asked one of Germany's leading literary editors about the state of culture there. "It is a disaster," was the answer. Over two-thirds of the books published are translations. This year's bestseller is a feminist fairy tale, *Good Girls Go to Heaven*. In his novel *Exemplary Lives*, a quarter of a century ago, Siegfried Lenz explained that, in view of their past, Germans could no longer decide what were right or wrong choices. Günter Grass believed that Hitler was not a matter of choice at all, but some kind of spell. German identity is the overwhelming topic. The likes of Hans Magnus Enzensberger or Martin Walser are serious about it; the plays or films of Fassbinder and Herzog and Heiner Müller and Peter Weiss are self-pitying. In half a century, there has been no controversy as intense as the *Historikerstreit*. What looked like an argument between historians about the reciprocities between Nazism and Communism was in fact commentary upon the national effort to forge a post-Hitler identity with which the Germans can live. How deep is the self-searching? Marcel Reich-Ranitski left his native Poland to become an influential literary critic. Lately, his former links with the Polish Communist secret police were exposed. All he could find to say in self-defense was that he owed the Germans no explanation. That was enough to quieten the scandal.

Umberto Eco, Leonardo Sciascia, Italo Calvino, managed to escape the sovietized stranglehold on Italian culture. Over three thousand literary prizes and festivals too numerous to be counted testify to local opportunity. In the window of the leading bookstore in Florence, though, the novels on sale were by Alison Fell, David Lodge, Patricia Highsmith, José Saramago, Kenzaburo Oe, Michael Crichton, Sten Nadolñy, John Fullerton, Peter Mayle, and finally an Italian, Romano Battaglia, with *Alle Porte della Vita.*

In Paris, I was unable to find a single painter or sculptor with an international reputation. Over ten years ago, Milan Kundera confessed to nostalgia for Paris but could not help seeing it as "the disappearing capital of a disappearing world." The current crop of Gallimard novels are by Jean-Denis Bredin, François-Régis Bastide, Daniel Pennac, Alina Reyes, Dominique Rolin, Gilles Coupet, Anna Wiazemsky, Patrick Modiano, and Jean d'Ormesson (whose title, *Presque rien sur presque tout*, seems to sum up the situation).

The June 1996 issue of the NRF carries lead articles about two Americans, Jack Kerouac and Jerome Charyn, followed by a section "L'Algérie des écrivains." The conclusion of an essay about Algerian intellectuals by the well-reputed Muhammad Dib is characteristic (the translation is mine): "Included in a world of signs, figuring themselves as signs in the great concert of signs, they communicate only through signs, not often understandable, and under the influence of the spread, more or less increased, or diminished, of the slightest oscillation." Perhaps applauded in the *hautes écoles*, this is hardly going to scare off the Islamic fundamentalists putting Algeria through fire. Virtually nothing is left of this former powerhouse (or of Otto Abetz's other three, come to that). That same month, *L'Infini*, a rival highbrow journal, had a lengthy essay on Francis Bacon by Philippe Sollers, once himself an editor, and then a story by David Bowie, once a pop singer. This concerned the dismemberment of a fourteen-year-old, and the translator and editor praised it as "authentically criminal art."

Britain is a still stranger swirl of prank and perversity. A London art gallery recently removed its roof in order to winch down some sheep whose fleece had been dyed pink. Elsewhere a young actress lay naked in a glass box for a week. For cementing a house, someone else was awarded a prestigious prize. Another bright hope has filled a gallery with thousands of shapes in human form, cut from tin or waste paper, all of them being swept away by dummy cleaners into litter bags.

Excrement is treated as one among other pigments. Helen Chadwick's *Piss Flowers* were cast from stains left where she had urinated on snow. Dinos and Jake Chapman have made a film in which two women fellate the penis-shaped nose of a decapitated mannequin. In a gallery, this same pair exhibit figures of children who are naked and hideously mutant, Siamese twinned randomly, with penis-noses, anus-mouths and vagina-chests. Damien Hirst, a young artist in vogue for sawing a cow in half, delivers himself of profundities in a quality Sunday newspaper: "I like taking my clothes off. I have a lot of friends who are like that, do you know what I mean? Pissing, shitting. Getting our dicks out. I guess we're just like weeping babies underneath." Hirst's cow was exhibited among other British sculptures in Paris, prompting the organizer of this show to reflect, "What strikes me most is this tremendous strength British sculptors have, which is the ability to banish the notion of tastefulness."

Blasted, a play staged at the Royal Court, was summed up by one critic with the words: "Seedy journalist has sex with retarded girl; soldier rapes back, then eats his eyes; and all in a hotel in Leeds during a civil war." This playwright's latest offering is an "improvement" of a classical Greek theme. Hippolytus, as one reviewer put it,

> is a terminal depressive who spends his time eating burgers, watching junk television and masturbating into his socks. Phaedra nevertheless gets the hots for this deeply unfanciable representative of Generation X, and administers oral sex. The recipient is so bored that he just carries on eating. Theseus rapes his daughter to enthusiastic cheers. Hippolytus has his penis cut off and grilled on a barbecue.

In remotest rural Wales, where the population is composed of sheep-farmers and has not increased in size since 1300, a theater company put on *Vagina Dentata*. This play, according to the local newspaper, begins with three women shooting the only male character, supposedly the writer and director of the play. A spokesman claimed, "It's like Chekhov on speed. It's a post-modern tragedy that plays with itself." Summoned in aid like this, a great writer is also diminished.

All Ways Six Steps is a modern dance that the choreographer Sasha Waltz staged as a part of a festival in London. Its setting is a bedroom. As the Sunday *Times* critic describes, "A Peter Pan creature floats in, so amoral that he tries to flatten Waltz (whom he has just married) between the upturned bed and wall, and, failing that, to squash her into a drawer. Another sinister young man also radically rearranges the furniture, balancing the armchair and dressing tables on the top edge of the walls. None of it makes sense, but then it's not meant to. I'd happily see it again."

Awarded for the first time this year, and worth thirty thousand pounds, the Orange Prize is restricted to women writers. Its winner, Helen Dunmore, was praised for "a hypnotic story of incest in the English countryside." The Betty Trask prize, hardly less valuable, is for romantic fiction. Graham Lord, one of its judges this year, complained at what he had to read. One novel concerned a drunken young Scottish woman "in which we are treated to a suicide, an orgy, porn videos, masturbation, lots of vomiting and a scene in which our heroine wakes to find that the man she picked up the previous night has defecated on her stomach because she was too drunk to have sex." Another novel was *Marked for Life* in which "a tattooed all over homosexual is assaulted with a candle by his wife, whose mother lives with a lesbian lover. There's a lot of vomit in this one too." Louis Doughty's *Crazy Paving* was "awash with foul dialogue, graphic descriptions of masturbation, menstruation and vomiting." *Clever Girl*, by the twenty-eight-year-old Tania Glyde, mentions in the first few pages "a dog's sexual excitement, dildoes, various bodily fluids, child abuse, loveless sex, lavatory paper . . . and other things too crude to reprint."

Daily life, to be sure, offers examples for such art to imitate. One Paul Scarrott, for example, was reported to have died at the age of forty in a Spanish hospital after a drinking bout. In a single year, he had nineteen convictions in court and been jailed thirteen times for offenses at football matches. His specialities were carrying offensive weapons and inciting the crowd to violence. A young man arrested for urinating on the wall of my local police station thought it a full explanation to say to the magistrate, "I did it, that's all." The most popular of the BBC's radio programs has a breakfast show. Its presenter, a young man, used to have a slot, "I'm in bed with my boyfriend." Lately, he rounded on a guest with the sentence, "Anthea, how about we get together while I kick you in the mouth?"

Many consider that the case for decadence is proven. Some years ago the philosopher Alasdair MacIntyre was already warning that Britain stood on the brink of moral illiteracy, so that a concept such as "good" or "just" was becoming inapplicable. In the opinion of Robert Harris, a popular author who is also a leading columnist, Britain "is becoming dumber as well as coarser." The historian and commentator Paul Johnson speaks of the country's proletarianization, whereby the young are dragged down into "the gutter culture," degraded by those who ought to know better. An official report on standards of education states that many seven-year-olds are unable to read; they seem likely to be functionally illiterate adults. Another report finds that nearly half those aged between eleven and fifteen never pick up a book. Students no longer understand an allusion to the Bible or the classics. A high court judge, a woman too, publicly suggested that marriage had outlived its usefulness. Selling in millions, the tabloid newspapers hero-worship assorted drug addicts and hooligans, pop stars and television personalities, sports figures, chefs, models, and designers.

Popular culture displays what Matthew Arnold described as "the plain faults of our animality." He foresaw the anarchy in which "this man and that" can "smash as he likes." In a society apparently indifferent to choice, artistico-smashers are able to express themselves only in a competition of shock. Assertion replaces fulfillment. Lifestyle replaces responsibility. That admired tastelessness is the tantrum of the infant against the arrangements of the daycare center.

Neither life nor art can do anything with infantilism. Within living memory, the critic made it his business to build a reef—in an image of Desmond MacCarthy's—that protects the lagoon of literature from the restless sea of nonsense and confusion. Whether out of fear to be unfashionable or from loss of moral authority, critics even come to praise what they hate. That is a novelty. Here, for instance, is the distinguished chairman of the Arts Council, once a poet, reviewing some new fiction. "I do not wish anyone to be dismembered by a chainsaw, raped, have their head smashed in a football game, to engage in bestiality or to be sodomized by a mad mortuary attendant seconds after their demise." All this, he continues, is here "conducted with such brio, and with so much narrative pace and accuracy of ear that his book is both revolting and exhilarating." By chance today, as I write, *The Times* has another equally routine example. The critic says that while here is "the first novel that made me physically sick, it is also one that held my attention utterly rapt." This fiction about a serial killer of young homosexuals is praised for its color, texture, wit, intelligence, and so on. A whole lexicon of critic's adjectives—shocking, irreverent, outrageous, relevant, provocative, disturbing, challenging—are the equivalent of mental-health warnings.

Disturbed as they are, bereft of moral authority, in cultural disarray, the populations of Europe are now caught inescapably in yet another collectivizing experiment. Over the last four or five decades, a handful of politicians, the Germans and French to the fore, have been organizing among themselves the formation of a federal structure, ultimately a single state structure, for all the countries of Europe. A capital in Brussels, a limited and unrepresentative parliament with power to spend but not yet to tax, a budget raised from contributions by national governments, not one but two European courts of justice with powers to override national courts, a president and a score of commissioners who are not elected but self-appointed, and ten thousand bureaucrats, are already in place. Centralized decision-making by officials is replacing democratic legislation. A bewildering torrent of directives and regulations control and standardize every aspect of daily life and commerce. In an invisible and usually whimsical tangle of wheeling and dealing, careers, fortunes, industries, whole regions thrive or fail. Irrespective of historic experience, law, language, or tradition, the nation-state is to become extinct, and all by decree.

Pan-European or vaguely Esperantist visions date from the last century. At the outset, the model for the present arrangement no doubt had idealistic impulses to avoid any repeat of war, but it came out of the matrix of Nazism and Communism with many conscious or unconscious borrowings.

"The United States of Europe" was the title of an article Leon Trotsky wrote for *Pravda* a few years after the 1917 revolution. European countries would unite in a socialist federation, he believed, as a prelude to a world socialist federation. This remained Soviet doctrine.

A construct superimposed by political will, federal Europe is a mimicry of the old Soviet Union in many respects. Those who set up its institutions were also believers in state control and protectionism. Whether at political or financial levels, politicians and their officials are not held accountable. There is no proper auditing. Billions of dollars, probably as much as a third of the entire Brussels budget, goes missing. Venality in the form of subsidies, tax credits, perks, bribes, and horse-trading has long since eroded idealism. An unprecedented number of leading European politicians and businessmen are in prison or on trial for corruption. Those operating the complex central system form a nomenklatura uncannily resembling those who lately were rich and privileged solely through membership in the Communist Party.

As also in the old Soviet Union, independent nations of different cultures and languages are to federate on a basis ideologically predetermined for them. This construct is artificial, an act of pure political will. Naturally people try to defend their historic identity, and the resulting backlash of nationalism, xenophobia, and racism excites the very horrors that federalism is supposed to exclude. Separatist groups everywhere are ready and willing to resort to violence in what is seen as defense of the nation and its culture. Ancient ghosts stir. Federal Europe is reproducing the defect that above all others put paid to the Soviet Union.

Since 1940, the Franco-German relationship has been guilty, not to say sadomasochistic. "In Europe, Germany alone decides," Hitler declared in August 1942, and he further asked of the French, "Can we absorb them with advantage?" In his view, the so-called New Order was to be a federal structure in which France would provide goods and

David Pryce-Jones

services. In September 1943, with Hitler's consent, Albert Speer and the French Minister of Production, Jean Bichelonne, set up a planning council as a preliminary toward an economically integrated Europe. Ambassador Otto Abetz was arguing that the French ought to be equal partners. The question, he explained to Bertrand de Jouvenel, is "whether you will proceed of your own free will."

Germans of all sorts, from Nazi intellectuals like Carl Schmitt and Werner Best to Ernst Jünger and some of the 1944 conspirators against Hitler, were writing reports to define the New Order. Among several Nazi think tanks working to that end was the so-called Society for European Economic Planning, under Werner Daitz, an associate of Alfred Rosenberg. SS General Otto Ohlendorf created the think tank in the Ministry of Economics that came closest to projecting what could actually occur. Although he was responsible for mass murder in Russia (and hanged for it after the war), Ohlendorf was an intellectual, a trained economist. He argued that a Nazi economic order would have to reconcile a free market with the state's role as main contractor and purveyor.

Correspondingly, thoughtful French collaborators saw convergence or alliance with Germany as the sole effective way to overcome defeat. *Anthologie de la nouvelle Europe* was an influential book edited by Alfred Fabre-Luce and published in 1942. Force was admirable, he argued in a lengthy Introduction, and Nazi aims were sound, though limited as they stood. For the sake of a higher form of European supremacy, France and Germany would have to sacrifice national sovereignty—it was a way of seeming to de-Nazify without actually doing so, merely taking out the racial sting. "Will Germany show itself worthy of the European task?" Fabre-Luce asked. "It is a question of engaging

France and Germany in a common enterprise to affirm their solidarity." As the war ended, he was arrested for the sentiment.

Unification in 1989 seemed like a civilian return to German primacy on the continent. Chancellor Kohl and his aides repeat ever more insistently that Germany must be locked into a federal Europe and tied down, or else it will revert to its bad old ways. Entrenched by now, the French instinct is to disarm potentially hostile strength by acquiring a share in it. Through the Maastricht treaty, both countries finalized committment to a common enterprise. The treaty embodies what its French critics openly call "the spirit of Vichy." Where once Hitler and Pétain shook hands, Chancellor Kohl and President Mitterand stood side by side holding hands. German tanks once again drove down the Champs Elysées, though only in a parade. In a final presidential speech, in Berlin, Mitterand praised the bravery of German soldiers in the war, and, in a posthumously published book, discovered in Prussia the virtues of enlightenment. It is the New Order as envisioned by Ohlendorf and Fabre-Luce. In this perspective, Laval and others executed for treason were simply premature Euro-fanatics.

Europe has a Commissioner of Culture, a middle-ranking Spanish official, as it happens. What passes for European culture is nothing of the kind, but entertainment of a mass nature, consisting of football matches and other sporting events, television co-productions, the Eurovision song contest (in which the recent British entry was called "Ooh Aah Just a Little Bit"), lotteries, and other commercial or marketing promotions. As the legacies of Communism and Nazism work themselves out, a populist and collectivized welfare state of continental proportions looms, in which genuine choice is more and more restricted, culture more and more marginalized. Prosperity is promised in return. In the next few years, people will have to decide whether to consent to these plans of their political masters or reject them. In either case, they are likely to discover how much more ruin there is in Europe.

September 1996

A Dearth of Feeling

Anne Applebaum

V ENICE has the Piazza San Marco, Paris has the Eiffel
Tower, and now Prague has the Charles Bridge: wide
and pedestrianized, blackened with age—and suffused with
the spirit of capitalism. There are buskers and hustlers along
the bridge, and, every fifteen feet or so, someone is selling
very much what one would expect to find for sale in such
a postcard-perfect spot. Paintings of appropriately pretty
streets are on display, along with bargain jewelry, and
"Prague" key chains. Soviet military paraphernalia is for
sale, too: caps, badges, belt buckles, and little pins, tin
Lenin and Brezhnev images of the sort which Soviet school
children and Soviet veterans once wore on their respective
uniforms.

It is a familiar sight now, but still an odd one. After all,
most of the people buying these things are Americans and
West Europeans, people who would be sickened by the
thought of wearing a swastika. They see nothing wrong, on
the other hand, with sporting the hammer and sickle on a
T-shirt or a hat. It is a minor observation—but sometimes
it is through just such minor observations that a cultural
mood is best observed. Here, the lesson could not be more
clear: while the symbol of one mass murder fills us with
horror, the symbol of another mass murder makes us laugh.

There are other ways, both minor and less so, in which

the same phenomenon can be observed. Look, for example, at the use of the term "collaborator" in English: it is applied broadly and frequently to the leaders of Vichy France and other Nazi parties in Europe—but it is almost never attached to East European Communists like General Jaruzelski or Janos Kadar. Equally odd is the different sense of propriety that applies to Western statesmen visiting foreign graveyards. In 1994, Bill Clinton visited Minsk, and asked to visit the mass graves which lie in the woods of Kuropaty outside the city, the scene of a Stalinist massacre. The Belorussian leadership refused. The president went anyway (on the "unofficial" part of his trip) but where was the outcry? Where were the furious editorials and letters to the editor?

If there is a dearth of feeling among politicians, journalists, and Prague tourists that what happened in Eastern Europe was evil in some fundamental way, that is matched and multiplied in Western popular culture. The Cold War produced James Bond thrillers and cartoon Russians of the sort who appear in Rambo films, but nothing even approaching the attempted quality of *Schindler's List* or *Sophie's Choice*, or the mass popularity of the TV series "Holocaust." Steven Spielberg, probably Hollywood's leading director (like it or not), has chosen to make films about Japanese concentration camps (*Empire of the Sun*) and Nazi concentration camps, but not about Stalinist concentration camps. The latter don't catch the imagination in the same way.

As I say, these are all small things: slips of the tongue, lines in an article, the presence or absence of Hollywood films. But put them all together and they make a story. Intellectually, Americans and West Europeans know what happened in the Soviet Union. Solzhenitsyn has been published here; the revelations of the *glasnost* years received due publicity abroad. The information about what happened is widely available: most educated people know that Stalin killed, by means of mass murder and concentration camps, at least twice as many innocent people as Hitler—not because he was a "worse" or "more unique" dictator (that is a pointless debate if there ever was one) but because he was in power much longer. He and his henchmen had time to stage the purges in Russia and the artificial famine in Ukraine, the murder of one in ten Balts and the near-liquidation of the Crimean Tartars, as well as the Katyn massacres, the Vinnitsa massacres, the Kuropaty massacres, among thousands of others. They also had time to plan educational and judicial systems which were designed to alter human nature and to erase historical memory—and in some cases succeeded. They even had time to foment civil wars in Africa, Asia, and Latin America as well. Hitler had time only for one attempted genocide, although he planned others.

And yet—Cold War propaganda notwithstanding—almost no one in the West feels these crimes to have been evil in the same, visceral way that they feel Hitler's crimes to have been evil. No one feels that the system itself was based on inhumane principles, or upon a fundamental misunderstanding of human nature. Ken Livingstone, a British MP who is a leading light of what is now referred to as "Old Labor" (as opposed to New Labor, led by Tony Blair), recently struggled to explain the difference to me. Yes, the Nazis were "evil," he said. But the Soviet Union was "deformed." That view echoes the feeling that many people have, even people who are not Old Labor, even people who think of themselves as "conservative" or "right-wing": the

27

Soviet Union simply went wrong somehow, but it was not fundamentally wrong in the way that Hitler's Germany was wrong. The ideas were good—it was the people who failed.

Until recently, it was possible to explain this lack or absence of popular feeling about the tragedy of European Communism as the logical result of a particular set of circumstances. The passage of time is part of it: Communist regimes did grow less reprehensible as the years went by. Nobody was really frightened of General Jaruzelski, or even Brezhnev. The absence of hard information, backed up by archival research, is clearly part of it too: the paucity of academic work on this subject was long due to a paucity of sources. There were no journalists to record the Siberian camps, as there were journalists in Cambodia during the Pol Pot regime. There were no television cameras to film the victims, as there were in Germany after the Second World War.

But ideology twisted the ways in which we understood Soviet and East European history as well. A small part of the Western Left struggled to explain and sometimes to excuse the purges from the 1930s onwards: even in the 1980s, there were still academics (for some reason, they often tended to be British academics) who went on describing the advantages of East German health care or Polish peace initiatives. The fact of the matter was that the founding philosophers of the Western Left were the same as those of the Soviet Union. Some of the language was shared as well: Marx and Engels, the masses, the struggle, the proletariat, the exploiters and exploited, the ownership of the means of production, and more. To condemn the Soviet Union too thoroughly would be to condemn a part of what the Western Left held dear.

The Western Right, on the other hand, did struggle to condemn Soviet crimes, but sometimes in an unhealthy way: surely the man who did the greatest damage to the cause of anti-Communism was Senator McCarthy. Recent documents showing that some of his suspicions were correct don't change the fact that the main effect of his overzealous pursuit of Communists in the American political establishment was to tarnish the cause of anti-Communism with the brush of chauvinism and intolerance forever. Even what ought to be the most basic, universally accepted assertion—"Communism was evil"—sounds, to the modern ear, "McCarthyite": simplistic and jingoistic and almost ignorant.

Of course, many of our current attitudes are also a fading by-product of the World War II alliance. For if Stalin was even half as bad as Hitler, that reflects rather badly on us: in effect, it is unacceptable to say that we defeated one genocidal criminal with the help of another. To admit that by sending thousands of Russians to their death by forcibly repatriating them after the war—or by consigning millions of people to Soviet rule at Yalta—the Western allies might have participated in war crimes on a vast scale would have undermined the legitimacy of the entire war effort. To admit that Churchill, at least, knew perfectly well what had happened to the Polish officers at Katyn (he denied it at the time) and guessed with some accuracy what was going to happen to East Europeans after the war is to admit that the war was not fought for moral reasons at all. If we admit that Stalin was the moral equivalent of Hitler, that makes some of those old photographs—Churchill, Stalin, and Roosevelt together—look damaging, almost terrifying now.

All of which is logical, but all of which is now old. In

the wake of the collapse of the Communist regimes in Eastern Europe, it seemed to me, as it did to many people, that this form of moral fuzziness, this dismissing of uncomfortable facts, would disappear. I had thought that our old ways of thinking about the Soviet Union would crumble along with the Berlin Wall, that anti-anti-Communism would disappear along with the Warsaw Pact. Freed of ideological constraints, of the legacy of McCarthyism, of memories of a wartime alliance with a country which no longer exists, with new access to archives and survivors' stories, we would at last be able to think and write about what happened in Eastern Europe with some degree of objectivity, some understanding of the depth of the experiment with human nature which was conducted there, and the horrors that it produced. I was wrong: ideology twists our recollections of that past now more than before, not less. And it looks set to go on doing so.

Perhaps it should come as no surprise that the moral confusion about the past is at its worst, and at its most damaging, in the former territories of the Communist world. This was not always the case: during the 1980s, when *glasnost* was just beginning in Russia, gulag survivors' memoirs sold millions of copies, and a new revelation about the past could sell out a newspaper. But more recently, history books containing similar "revelations" are badly reviewed in Russia—a new biography of Lenin, based for the first time on archival material, was dismissed by critics as "uninteresting"—or ignored. "People don't want to hear any more about the past," I was told last year by Lev Rozgon, the author of one of the most popular Russian survivors' accounts. "People are tired of the past."

Since then, survivors' accounts have become harder to

find, while archives from Vilnius to Vladivostok are closing their doors. Even historians need to eat, and there is more money to be made serving as an interpreter for a Western bank. The survivors themselves are ignored. In Poland, the society of "Siberiaks," the survivors of Siberian concentration camps, is a small and unimportant organization, without much money or national presence. In Russia, Memorial, the group which has dedicated itself to documenting and publishing the history of the gulag, is weak, underfunded and divided, and remains far from the center of public debate.

If there is little attention paid to the written memorials, there are few physical memorials either. In Siberia there are almost none at all. At Vorkuta, where hundreds of thousands died in the mines, the barracks are still inhabited: when the camp was closed, there was nowhere else for ex-guards and ex-prisoners to go. In other parts of Siberia, camp buildings have simply faded back into the forest, unmarked and unremembered. In *Imperium*, his book about Russia, Ryszard Kapuscinski describes his attempt to leave flowers in Vorkuta, in remembrance of the dead:

[I] wanted to place them somewhere, but I didn't know where. I thought, I'll stick them into some snowdrift, but there were people everywhere, and I felt that doing so would be awkward. I walked farther, but on the next street, the same thing: many people. Meanwhile, the flowers were starting to freeze and stiffen. I wanted to find an empty courtyard, but everywhere children were playing. I worried that they would find the carnations and take them . . . so I went beyond the town limits, and there, calmly, I placed the flowers amid the snowdrifts.

In some East European cities, it is possible to find the occasional, usually very modest, memorial. In one Warsaw suburb, a historically minded priest has put up an impressive, and very moving, monument to the victims of Communism, and there are one or two others in the city. In Moscow, there is a small sculpture in front of the Lubyanka, the prison through which thousands of people passed on their way east—but nothing on the scale of the immense monuments to the Great Victory in the Great Patriotic War. In Prague, there is a monument to Jan Palach's self-immolation, where visitors can lay flowers. In Vilnius, people leave flowers beneath a plaque which hangs outside the old KGB headquarters.

But these efforts often seem small and scattered, and they are countered by examples of post-Communist authorities refusing to put up monuments, too. The Belorussian government has refused to devote any resources to building a monument at Kuropaty. The Russian government is also hampering the construction of a full-fledged Polish cemetery in Katyn, on the grounds that it is unnecessary to commemorate the deaths of a few Poles when so many Russians died. Along with this refusal—how quickly things come full circle—the rewriting process has begun. A new book, *The Katyn Detective Story*, has recently been circulating among Russian parliamentarians. It contends that the Katyn murders were committed by the Nazis, not by the Soviet Union, and describes the dead officers as "aggressive idiots," servants of a Polish state which was little more than a "gluttonous European prostitute."

But what really marks the difference between postwar Germany and post-Communist Eastern Europe is not the lack of photographs and the lack of historical memory and the lack of monuments: it is the lack of any public discussion of guilt. A decade has passed since the first glimmerings of *perestroika* and the first, tentative debate about the more distant past—the 1930s in the old Soviet Union, the 1950s in Eastern Europe. So far, only a handful of people have actually been put on trial—or called to account in any way for the crimes of the past.

Leaving aside the question of ordinary Communists or ordinary informers (of whom there are thousands), there are, at large in Eastern Europe and elsewhere, people who qualify as actual war criminals: men who were directly responsible for organizing mass murders, or for helping to carry them out. Until recently, most of the men who carried out the Katyn massacres were still alive. Before he died, the KGB conducted an interview with one of them, asking him to explain how the murders were carried out, from a technical point of view. Last year, the Russian security services presented it to the cultural attaché of the Polish embassy in Moscow. There was never any suggestion that the man on tape should have been returned to Warsaw for trial.

True, there have been one or two highly publicized trials and arraignments: a few East German border guards, a KGB chief in Latvia, a Czech Stalinist who assisted the Russian invasion of 1968. In Poland, a handful of small trials have been carried out, attracting little attention. The trial of Adam Humer, a man accused of brutal torture during the brief Stalinist era, has received only the briefest notices in the press. Perhaps that was why, when confronted with one of his victims, an elderly woman, he felt perfectly comfortable replying, "Shut up, you old bitch." In Russia, where admittedly the problem of the guilty is vast—the Russian republic is still the home of Stalinist prosecutors who sent millions to die—there has not even been a symbolic trial, a

33

mini-Nuremburg, an attempt to point a finger at anyone in particular.

It can be argued that such trials are not a wholly successful way of dealing with the past, nor are they easy to carry out. The Nuremburg trials themselves were fraught with corruptions and contradictions (not the least of which was the presence of Soviet judges who knew perfectly well that their own side was also responsible for mass murder). In the years after the war, West Germany also brought more than eighty-five thousand Nazis to trial, but obtained fewer than seven thousand convictions. The tribunals which examined the cases were notoriously corrupt, and easily swayed by personal jealousies and disputes—although few would argue, in retrospect, that they should not have been carried out at all.

It can also be argued that it is too late for most Stalinist prosecutors to stand trial. Those who committed their crimes before the war are almost certainly all dead, those who were responsible for the deportations of the 1940s are very old. Nuremburg took place directly after the war, when the perpetrators of terrible crimes still, figuratively, had blood on their hands. Of course, this argument would be anathema to Simon Wiesenthal, to the Israelis who put Eichmann on trial in 1961, and even to British prosecutors, who have recently arrested an elderly Belorussian, Szymon Serafimowicz, under the British War Crimes Act, passed in 1991. Even Steven Spielberg, when asked why he made *Schindler's List*, replied, "I was afraid of the world my children were being raised in, that something like the Holocaust could happen to them." It is a sentiment that many, rightly, share.

Certainly it is also true that—if the comparison is to be made—the Germans themselves were not, during the twenty years after the end of the war, very eager to discuss the Nazi past either. Yet in postwar Germany, Nazi memorabilia was illegal, the Nazi Party was banned—and it has never revived on any large scale. The German state paid enormous reparations to individual Jews (if not always to others) and to the state of Israel. While the Germans may not have talked much about the war in public, official histories of the war were published, monuments were constructed. Everyone knew about Nuremburg; the groundwork was laid for the younger generation to discover the past. By the 1960s—sparked, in fact, by the trial of Auschwitz guards—when the national debate finally began, at least it was possible for the children of Nazis to discover what their parents had done. By the 1980s, the past had almost become a national obsession: hardly an evening passed when there wasn't a documentary or a talk show on German television dealing with the war.

In Eastern Europe, by contrast, Communist symbols and songs are not banned. Communist parties are not banned everywhere either. On the contrary, although the laws vary from country to country, in many places Communist parties have been allowed to retain their (sometimes enormous) assets: buildings, foreign bank accounts, membership lists, cars, and homes. Retired Communist Party members continue to receive outsize pensions. No other political party can match their material wealth: no other political parties existed in Eastern Europe before 1989. Partly as a result, in Poland, in Hungary, in Bulgaria, in Lithuania, and in Russia, well-funded former Communist parties are enjoying a revival; in many countries, they have slowly come to dominate the political scene. Communism has been discussed, but not condemned; Communists have been denounced in the heat of political campaigns, but not put to trial by the judicial system. No groundwork is being laid for the next generation to discover, or to condemn, their oppressive behavior in the past.

Oddly enough, the only systematic attempts to make an official condemnation of the past have occurred in Central Europe, and have involved not Stalinist criminals but petty bureaucrats, and not trials but vetting procedures. At issue was "lustration": the opening of files which contained names of former secret-police informers. Vigorous debates about lustration took place in Poland, Hungary, Czechoslovakia, and East Germany, among others—although in none of those countries were the aims of lustration very broad. Arguments about lustration mainly revolved around the question of whether it was proper for high-ranking officials, particularly elected officials, to go on serving if they had carried out extensive deceptions in the past—and whether the public should have access to the secret files which still contain extensive records of their day-to-day activities. Corruption was also at issue, along with the need for openness: among other things, the interior ministry files in most post-Communist countries contain evidence of which Communist leaders stole what money, and how.

Frequently, debates about lustration degenerated into debates about the past—which was hardly surprising: the past had not been discussed or expiated in any other way. Issues sometimes merged. Without any memorials, without any camp monuments, without any trials, many Central Europeans came to expect too much of lustration; many believed that lustration would help clear the air altogether, that it would provide a solution both to the nagging sense that the more distant, Stalinist crimes had not been punished, and to more recent memories of spying and petty theft. Perhaps as a result of these high expectations—and the depth of the objections—the lustration debate in Poland was so vicious that it brought down the first, fully elected democratic government; in Hungary, it was no less controversial. Curiously, in both countries the strongest case against lustration was made not by former Communists, but by former dissidents. Mostly, they seem to have feared what it would reveal about their opposition movements: Adam Michnik, a Polish dissident who was allowed to look at his friends' files soon after the fall of Communism (an anomaly of the sort created by the failure to give equal access to the files: why Michnik? why not others?), emerged shocked at how many of his old colleagues had in fact been informers, as he has since told many people. He later led the fight against lustration.

Elsewhere, of course, files were kept closed for more obvious reasons. Former Communists object to lustration for the same reason that they object to trials of Stalinists and monuments to Stalinist crimes: they object because they do not want to confess to their own guilt, or do not want to be associated with the crimes of others. Boris Yeltsin is only one of hundreds of former Soviet politicians who fall clearly into this category.

In the end, only the Czech and East German governments succeeded in passing such a law: in both countries, it is possible for ordinary citizens to get hold of their own files. In the Czech Republic, it is also the case that people who had previously worked as informers or as high-ranking Communists cannot hold elected office. In Germany, some high-ranking former Communists have also lost their jobs. The results are there to see: although in most of the Eastern block, the political scene is dominated by former Communists, that is not the case in either the Czech Republic or former East Germany.

But if the collapse of the Berlin Wall in 1989 did not bring about a reassessment of the legacy of the Communist past in former Communist parts of Europe, the transformation in the West was no less incomplete. The lack of moral certainty where Soviet crimes are concerned was always academic, as well as popular. For example, until five or ten years ago, Robert Conquest, author of *The Great Terror*, was often considered a paranoid alarmist for claiming that Stalin had murdered millions of people, when most history books spoke of hundreds: certainly I was taught as much when studying Russian history at Yale in the mid-1980s. His views are, of course, now mainstream: they are supported by archival evidence, to the limited extent that such evidence is now available, and by Soviet historians.

And yet—the opposite view persists as well. Legitimate academics, with prestigious jobs at prestigious universities, can write books which amount to "gulag denial," and nobody finds their writing either offensive or objectionable. J. Arch Getty, of the University of California, Riverside—famous for having written that "thousands" died in the gulag—goes on teaching and writing as always, but there are younger ones, too. Robert W. Thurston, a tenured professor at Miami University, recently wrote a book called *Life and Terror in Stalin's Russia, 1934–1941*, published by the equally reputable Yale University Press. In it he suggests, among other things, that the great purge took place without Stalin's knowledge, that it was supported by many people, and that, by promoting upward mobility, it laid the foundations for *perestroika*. Aside from getting many of his facts wrong—see Conquest's list of them in his review in the *Times Literary Supplement* ("Small

Terror, few dead," May 31, 1996)—Thurston seems unable, throughout the book, to understand the absurdity of what he is saying. After all, the same could be said (once again) of Hitler's Germany: Hitler was voted into power, after all; there is no proof he knew about the Holocaust; and under his regime many young, enthusiastic people came to power much earlier than they would have done otherwise. None of which amounts to a defense of a regime that also murdered millions of people.

Most of the "interest" in the book partly derives, of course, from the fact that it is different, that it purports to offer an opposite idea, a new perspective. This point of view—the idea that there is still "another side to the story," that not to acknowledge it would be "one-sided"—persists in the less genteel world of journalism as well. Not long ago, I was told by the editor of the *London Review of Books* that a review I had written of David Remnick's *Lenin's Tomb* could not be printed because it was too anti-Soviet. When I pointed out that the book itself was not exactly pro-Soviet, she replied that if that were the case, the book would not be reviewed. It wasn't.

In the West, a similar, and closely related, argument has also been mounted against those East Europeans who want to examine—and to condemn—the behavior of Communist regimes. This point was most eloquently put in a book which recently won the National Book Award in the United States as well as a Pulitzer Prize: *The Haunted Land* by Tina Rosenberg, who now writes editorials for *The New York Times*. Rosenberg does a good job at carefully enumerating the many complexities and drawbacks of lustration and war crimes trials. However, she then comes to the conclusion that, while trials are fine for Latin American dictators, they are not acceptable for East Europeans. Her reasoning depends partly upon the distinction, common among Western intellectuals, between the evil aims of most dictatorships, and the good intentions of Communism: "Communism's ideas of equality, solidarity, social justice, an end to misery, and power to the oppressed are indeed beautiful," in her own words. Here it is again: the ideas were fine, it is the people who failed. That the ideas were wrong still escapes her; that Hitler had ideals, too, is also not mentioned.

But most of Rosenberg's argument—like the arguments of others in the Western and Eastern media who feared an anti-Communist "witch hunt"—emphasizes the fragility of civil society in the newly democratic societies of Central and Eastern Europe. Condemnation of the past, she feared, could degenerate into violations of civil liberties, into persecution of innocent people, into moral self-righteousness and (figurative) burnings at the stake. What she appears to be afraid of is resurgent "nationalism" of a 1930s sort, perhaps in the form of an "anti-Communist right-wing." Even the title of her book, like the title of so many books written about the region recently, gives the idea away: Central Europe is "the haunted land" in her words, dogged by the prewar past, just as the lands of ex-Yugoslavia are filled with Robert Kaplan's "Balkan ghosts."

But the problem with modern Eastern Europe is not the legacy of the 1930s: the problem with Eastern Europe is the legacy of Communism, whether in the form of corruption, poverty, pollution, ill-health, or distorted values. Equally, the real danger to democracy and capitalism in Poland or Russia is not some form of warmed-over fascism, but Communist ideals, the Communist economic legacy, and the corrupt habits of former Communists themselves. Almost every time a regime has gone sour in the former Communist bloc over the past five years—in Serbia most notably, but in Slovakia as well, for example—the root cause is not some group of new nationalists, but former Communists wearing new clothes. As for the region disintegrating into an anti-Communist uproar, precisely the opposite has occurred. There have been very few unjust prosecutions of former Communists in the region, because there have been hardly any prosecutions of any kind.

In fact, Rosenberg's argument, like that of Thurston or Getty, appears to be rooted not in actual observation of life in Central Europe, but in a deep desire to protect the legacy of the Western Left, again in her words, "Communism's ideas of equality, solidarity, social justice, an end to misery, and power to the oppressed." Perhaps not coincidentally, she has also defended Thurston in print, in an odd little article in *The New York Times Book Review*. In the course of denouncing David Irving, the Nazi apologist, and arguing that his book should not be published by a reputable publisher, she applauds the decision of the Yale University Press to publish Thurston, the Stalin apologist, on the grounds that challenging and controversial ideas, even if they amount to gulag denial, deserve to see the light of day. Again, her argument only makes sense if we assume that only one version of totalitarianism and mass murder this century deserves a moral condemnation, while others ought to be treated as neutral historical phenomena. It only makes sense if we assume that there was, within Communism, something "good" which can still be rescued and brought to light, whereas there was no such "good" to be found in Hitler's Germany. In other words, it doesn't make sense at all.

But does it matter? Does the existence of popular and

highly regarded journalists and academics who play down the terror and distortions of Communism make any difference to us? Does the failure to condemn, or even to think about the past, matter to the Central Europeans either?

Alas, it does. Look first, again, at the former Communist bloc: the most obvious danger to civil society in the region is not that posed by non-existent anti-Communists. The real fear is now what the absence of lustration or the absence of official condemnation of the past might do to civil society, and to popular awareness of concepts like "justice" and "public morality."

Compare, once again, the role of history in the politics of postwar Germany and the politics of post-Soviet Russia. In modern Germany, the awareness of guilt—the memory of the Second World War—continues to matter tremendously to German politicians. Even in the years before the flowering of popular memory, this was the case. Germany's commitments to NATO, and to the European community, both derive from German politicians' fears of repeating the past; Helmut Kohl, the German chancellor, has followed his predecessors and explicitly stated his desire to lock Germany permanently into a European superstate, the better to prevent Germany from misbehaving again. As recently as last year, the German parliament debated for weeks over whether to send peacekeeping troops abroad: the very thought of Germans in uniform outside Germany, for whatever purpose, was too much for many German politicians.

The Russian leadership feels no such qualms. If they really remembered—viscerally, emotionally remembered—that Stalin, in the name of Communism and Great Russian imperialism, deported tens of thousands of Chechens to Siberia, the inhabitants of the Kremlin would be unable blithely to drop bombs on civilians in Chechnya today, murdering forty thousand, or to announce a plan to "eliminate the Chechens like dogs," as Boris Yeltsin promised in the wake of one recent Chechen hostage crisis.

The effects of the failure to remember the past elsewhere in Eastern Europe are less dramatic, but no less damaging. Take another comparison: Poland and the Czech Republic. While they carried out their lustration program, the Czechs went through a very brief period of national obsession with spies, secret agents, and personal files. Many mistakes were made, as Tina Rosenberg recorded; some people who felt they were innocent were excluded from national politics (although not excluded from anything else). Some unattractive young people, none of whom had ever faced the decisions which their parents had faced, made use of lustration for their own political ends. Now the wave of interest in the subject has virtually disappeared (so much for the disruption of civil society which Rosenberg feared) but the stigma attached to Communism remains. As noted above, the Czech Republic is one of the few in Central Europe which has not elected former Communists back to power.

In Poland, on the other hand, the unopened files remain a hovering presence in political life. In January, the Polish prime minister, Jozef Oleksy, was forced to resign: he had been accused of having been a KGB spy, indeed of remaining a KGB spy after 1989. Originally, this information came from Lech Walesa, who was then the Polish president. Why did Mr. Walesa have privileged access to the files? What is the truth about Mr. Oleksy's position? Why were his Russian contacts not known before he became prime minister?

Nobody has answers. And so it will go in the future: the presence of secrets will weigh heavily on politicians, poisoning public life.

The return to dominance of elites who are associated with the totalitarian past will also have a profound impact on the shape of the economies of the Eastern bloc. Of course it might be argued that the former Communists are now merely a nascent bourgeoisie, which is to be applauded; and that is what the best of them indeed are. But it is not quite that simple. The evolution of a bourgeoisie is a healthy phenomenon when it grows and prospers thanks to bourgeois values: hard work, honesty, personal responsibility. What happens when you have a corrupt business class which is intimately entwined with a corrupt political class? You might still have a bourgeoisie, and you might still have capitalism, but they won't necessarily take the form that everyone would applaud.

For all the talk of liberalism and Thatcherism and free markets that took place in the region in 1989, the model which Central Europe will probably most closely resemble in the coming years is that of pre-Tangentopoli Italy. Whether the model is northern or southern Italy depends upon the country (Poland might be the former, Romania is perhaps the latter) but the idea is the same: there will be some forms of robust private entrepreneurship; an enormous, untaxed, grey market; and large companies, some state-owned and some private, which enjoy deeply corrupt relationships with powerful politicians. Various forms of criminal Mafia will dominate some parts of the region; politicians will come to "represent" various business interests, as they clearly do already, particularly in Russia. Some post-Soviet republics may, of course, slide further. Yegor

Gaidar once said that Russia faced the choice between aspiring to be like America, or being forced to become like Africa. But Latin America is an option, too: huge gaps between rich and poor, political violence, massive slums, perennially unstable fiscal and monetary policies.

Worse than the effect on politics and economics, though, is the effect which the denial of all guilt has on ordinary East Europeans themselves. Leaving aside the scandals which will continue to engulf successive regimes, leaving aside the lack of history which allows Mr. Yeltsin to behave as he does in the Caucasus, there is another way in which the resurgence of old elites will have a powerful impact on the politics of Eastern Europe in the future: if scoundrels of the old regime go unpunished, then good will in no way have been seen to triumph over evil. This may sound apocalyptic, but it is not politically irrelevant. The police do not need to catch all the criminals all the time for most people to submit to public order, but they need to catch a significant proportion. Nothing encourages lawlessness more than the sight of villains—even if they are merely people who took money for information, not concentration camp guards—getting away with it, living off their spoils, and laughing in the public's face.

For millions of people, the failure to condemn the past proves that it does not pay to be decent. Tina Rosenberg wrote that "under Communism, the lines of complicity ran like veins and arteries through the human body." But that was patently not the case: there were people who collaborated far more than others. And from the current perspective, it seems to most people that the more you collaborated, the wiser you were. Those who got ahead in the past have been able to keep their apartments, their dachas, and control of the businesses which they bought up on the cheap. Millions of ordinary people, who were never seduced by the ideology, never joined the Party for the sake of a career, simply look foolish. Honesty does not pay; corruption does. Those who work hard do not succeed, those who murder and bribe their way to power and prominence do.

Our failure in the West to understand the magnitude of what happened in Central Europe does not, of course, have the same profound implications for our way of life. Our tolerance for "gulag deniers" in our universities or admirers of Communism in our press will not destroy the moral fabric of our society: the Cold War is over, after all, and there is no real intellectual or political force left in the Communist or even the socialist parties of the West.

But there will be consequences. For one, our understanding of what is happening now in the former Soviet Union is distorted by our misunderstanding of history. Again, if we really felt—if we really, deeply felt—that what Stalin did to the Chechens amounted to genocide, it is not only Yeltsin who would be unable to do the same things to them now, but we who would be unable to sit back with any equanimity and watch him. In fact, our response to the shocking invasion of Grozny, to the murder of many thousands of people, has been to turn away and call it an internal Russian matter: there is even some evidence that American intelligence may have been used in the (unsuccessful) attempt to defeat the Chechens. The moral horror which we would have felt following a German invasion of Sudetenland in 1952, or which we do feel when we observe German neo-Nazism today, is simply not there in our attitudes to Russia.

Our approach to European security questions is distorted in similar ways. When Nazi Germany finally fell, the rest of the West mobilized in a way it never had done before, and may never do again. Both NATO and the European Community were created in part to cement Germany into the West, to prevent Germany from ever breaking away from civilized "normality" again. No such efforts have been made with either Central Europe or Russia. On the contrary: when the nations of Central Europe first petitioned to join NATO in 1991, the Bush administration treated them like unwanted guests. They were told to be quiet, to go home, to stop disrupting the world of "adult" diplomats and statesmen. There was no sense that they had a right to be afraid—even a right to be paranoid—about their national sovereignty, after the experience of forty years of occupation. Even now, as NATO membership for some Central European states begins to look feasible, it is still possible to meet Western ambassadors in Central European capitals who complain privately that NATO expansion is a "great bother," more trouble than it's worth.

Finally, though, if we go on accepting the idea that there are "multiple interpretations" of Soviet history, it is our own history which we will go on misunderstanding. Why did we fight the Cold War, after all? Was it because crazed right-wing politicians, in cahoots with the military-industrial complex and the CIA, invented the whole thing and forced two generations of Americans to go along with it? Or was there something more important happening? Was there a real ideological enemy, whose ideas and weapons really did threaten some of the most fundamental principles of our civilization, whose political aim was to destroy the West, and whose political achievements included the destruction of the economies and civil societies of half of the

European continent—Poland, Hungary, the Czech Republic, Slovakia, Bulgaria, Romania, Albania, Eastern Germany, the nations of Yugoslavia, the Baltic States, Russia, Belorussia, Ukraine, Moldova, Armenia, Azerbaijan, and Georgia—not to mention large parts of Africa and Asia as well?

I am afraid that it is only a matter of time before the former proposition begins to seem true: until, more and more, the Cold War seems like a joke got up by a few fanatics and "McCarthyites," the NATO alliance seems like an expensive bother, and the support for dissidents and human rights advocates in the former Soviet Union seems like the whim of a few ancient politicians with bees in their collective bonnets. Already, we are forgetting, very rapidly, what it was that mobilized us, what inspired us, what convinced our politicians to spend the billions which they undoubtedly did spend. Already, our elites are forgetting why the rest of the world still expects us to behave like a "moral" power, not merely a Machiavellian one.

The change is already happening. Not long ago, I was in California, the land of lost history, and listened to an educated acquaintance complain at great length about the amount of money which the Cold War cost: asked whether he would have preferred to see a Western Europe dominated by Communist regimes, he shrugged and said he didn't much mind. Five decades' worth of Western solidarity, carefully forged in the NATO alliance, a myriad of free-trade agreements, a thousand summits and conferences: all had disappeared. His sense that there is something called Western civilization, which needs, periodically, to be defended from challenges like the one once posed by Communism—that had disappeared too.

As long as Communism is not seen, along with National

Socialism, as one of the great ills of our century, Californians and others will grow more inclined to see the Cold War as a waste of time and the West as a fiction. In the end, it is we Americans who will not understand our past, we who will not understand why the world perceives us as it does, we who will not understand how our country came to be the way it is. In the end it is we who will wake up and realize that we do not know who we are.

October 1996

The Eclipse of Listening

Roger Scruton

MUSIC exists in every human society. In its primary forms of dance, march, and collective song, it is a participatory activity whose purpose is often religious or bellicose. The throbbing drum of the war dance is the spirit of the tribe, in which the warrior loses his identity so as to become one with the collective will. The hymn is the collective voice of the congregation as it communes with its god.

In Western civilization, music of a quite different kind has gradually pushed the old participatory forms to one side. Our musical culture depends on a radical divide between performer and listener. For us the act of listening takes place in silence, often in the hushed and reverential atmosphere of a concert hall. To sing, hum, gesticulate, or tap your feet in time is not just bad manners. It is a violation of the sacred ritual, which merits nothing less than expulsion from the divine presence into the cacophonous street outside.

Cultural historians have begun to ask themselves when this momentous transition from a participatory to a listening culture occurred. As James Johnson shows in *Listening in Paris* (1995), his brilliant examination of the growth of opera as a spectacle in eighteenth-century France, it was only by degrees that audiences learned to fall silent. The rise of the instrumental "concert" in the late Renaissance, and the very names of "sonata" and "symphony," suggest a gradual dawning of the new conception of music as sound that deserves attention for its own sake alone. Shakespeare's many beautiful invocations of the power of music suggest the wonder with which music was received by a man who had newly learned to put day-to-day interests aside, in order to listen.

The culture of listening has not been confined to Western civilization. We find parallels in India, Bali, and China. But an additional factor has enriched our musical experience. This is the discovery of tonality as a device for uniting the melodic and harmonic potential of every musical element. I call this a discovery, not just because it arose only in some parts of the world, but more importantly because, wherever it arose, it brought about an irreversible change in the way music was conceived. Before the arrival of tonality, music is confined to monodic melody, supported by rhythmic movement. There is no doubt that the monodic forms of music may achieve the greatest subtlety and invention —witness Gregorian chant and the Indian raga. But tonality brings with it a third dimension of development, so that music loses its free and improvisatory character—the character of linear movement—and finds itself bound by the laws of harmonic succession. Voices can now be combined, and the harmonic sequences that emerge from this have a logic of their own, constraining and constrained by the melodic line.

The death of tonality was prophesied by Arnold Schönberg, who then (like other modern prophets) attempted to produce the condition he foretold. In musicological circles it has become a cliché that tonality is a cliché—in other words, that its effects are empty, exhausted, and false. And if tonality collapses, what remains of the Western tradition?

How should we relate to the music of the past if its very language is no longer seriously usable, but usable only in inverted commas, as in David Del Tredici's *Final Alice*, or John Corigliano's postmodern opera *Last Days at Versailles*?

Although our musical culture has passed through a period of acute crisis, it does not seem to me that this crisis was caused either by the death of tonality, or by the rise of the atonal experiments that attempted to replace it. On the contrary, it was caused precisely by the *suspicion* of tonality —a suspicion that should be seen as part of the almost universal alienation of Western intellectuals from the legacy of bourgeois culture during the late nineteenth century. The suspicion of tonality, like Marx's suspicion of private property, or Sartre's suspicion of the bourgeois family, or the abstractionist suspicion of figurative painting, should be seen for what it is: an act of rebellion against the only way we have of making sense of things. The root cause of our musical crisis is the same as the root cause of so many other crises during our century: namely, the rise of the intelligentsia as a priesthood of unbelievers. The time has come for a reassessment of tonality and of the impetuous criticisms to which it has all but succumbed.

There is a tendency among ethnomusicologists to describe tonality as "Western tonality," implying that it is one idiom among many, of no universal significance. This attitude has been reinforced by modern compositional techniques, which attempt to retain polyphony while discarding the laws of tonal harmony. The "emancipation of the dissonance" that Schönberg announced has also been taken as the superseding of tonality. We have been encouraged to see tonality as a passing idiom whose authority is dependent upon a vanishing musical culture. But this attitude fails to do justice to the underlying appeal of tonal harmony.

The interesting thing is not that tonality arose in the West, but that its discoveries cannot be made available without being adopted—often, it is true, to the detriment of the local music culture (as in Indian Bunjee music), but always with a greedy sense that *this* is what music needs for its enrichment. For three hundred years, Japan remained cut off from Western art music, locked in its grisly imitations of the Chinese court orchestras, dutifully producing sounds as cacophonous to local ears as the croaking of jackdaws. Within a few decades of the Meiji restoration, young Japanese had all but forgotten their traditions and were playing Mozart and Beethoven on home-produced pianos with the same relish as their Western contemporaries, and dreaming of symphonies and concertos that they would add to the classical repertoire. Within half a century, the bamboo flute and the koto had become exotic addenda to the symphony orchestra.

Indeed, Western music is a symbol of Western civilization itself. It is the perfect expression of the "Faustian" spirit that Spengler identified as the prime mover of our achievements: the spirit of restless discovery, which must always go deeper into the cause and the meaning of things. Not without reason did Thomas Mann choose music as the preoccupation of his modern Dr. Faustus. And in endowing his hero with the despairing thought that tonality has exhausted itself, that nothing now remains for music but a "taking back" of its greatest utterances, Mann found the perfect symbol for his belief that Western civilization has at last come to an end.

Announcing its own demise has been such an enduring mark of Western civilization that we should approach

Mann's thesis with a measure of Faustian skepticism. The amazing fact is that, notwithstanding the attempted suicide of the First World War, the barbarism of Nazi Germany, and the malign nothingness of Communism, a kind of civilization endures in the Western hemisphere. True, it is a civilization without a religious heart, and many would agree with Spengler that its days are therefore numbered. Nevertheless, unlike the other civilizations whose remnants lie strewn across the battlefield of the twentieth century, it is still breathing. And one sign of this is that people listen to music, perform music for themselves and others, and discriminate between the works that we ought to listen to and those that we ought to avoid.

In this at least Thomas Mann was right: if we wish to gauge the health of Western civilization, then we should study its musical culture. How much remains of that tradition of listening, and with what ease and conviction are new works being added to its repertoire? When Schönberg first devoted his great intellect to the overthrow of tonality it was partly as a gesture of defiance toward the audiences of his day, whose habit of disrupting the concerts in which his innovative music was first performed showed how far the tacit understanding between composer and listener had already broken down. By 1946, Schönberg was writing as though the audience had no legitimate part to play in the creation and understanding of music, and as though it entered the equation only by overhearing a dialogue between the composer and his inner voice. In his essay titled "Heart and Brain in Music," Schönberg wrote that

> those who compose because they want to please others, and have audiences in mind, are not real artists. They are not the kind of men who are driven to say something

whether or not there exists one person who likes it, even if they themselves dislike it. They are not creators who must open the valves in order to relieve the interior pressure of a creation ready to be born. They are more or less skillful entertainers who would renounce composing if they did not find listeners.

It is as though the priest, disgusted with his sinful congregation, has turned his back on them, so as to communicate with God alone.

Schönberg's attitude to the audience is of a piece with his atonal music. Tonality, for Schönberg and his followers, had exhausted its potential, and its principal devices had "become banal." It was no longer possible for a composer seriously to make use of the tonal idiom, since to do so would be to compromise the demands of inner truthfulness, to play to the gallery, and to utter musical platitudes whose appeal to the uninstructed masses condemned them as unfit for spiritual consumption. In effect, the listening culture had turned against itself. By admitting too many to its precinct, the temple had been defiled.

With those thoughts, Schönberg helped to launch modern music on a course of self-destruction. For it was tonality, with its unique potential to synthesize the melody and the harmonic dimensions, that made counterpoint and voice-leading intelligible to the ordinary musical ear, and so made it possible for people not otherwise versed in musical theory to follow the argument of a symphony or a string quartet, and to understand the message addressed through tones to their emotions. Take away tonality, and you remove that which makes polyphony accessible to all but the experts. And an art addressed only to experts is an art detached from the culture that provides its frame of reference. It is a neurasthenic art, spectral and rarefied, cut off from the lifeblood that only an audience can renew.

Schönberg, as is well known, set out to find an alternative to tonal organization. He wrote:

> It is evident that abandoning tonality can be contemplated only if other satisfactory means for coherence and articulation present themselves. If, in other words, one could write a piece that does not use the advantages offered by tonality and yet unifies all elements so that their succession and relation are logically comprehensible.

This search for the "alternative," which began with atonal serialism, has led from one arcane experiment to another, to the point where the "logically comprehensible" is just that: comprehensible as logic, but not as music. It is possible for a mathematician, versed in set theory, to get a kick out of Milton Babbitt's ingenious permutations of hexachords. But how many fragments of Babbitt can be sung, whistled, or hummed with feeling? How many can be retained in the memory as music, or heard as polyphony is heard? The whole point of this music is that it should *not* be intelligible to the ordinary musical ear; it is there to create a barrier between the vulgar and the cognoscenti. The complaint is reasonably made, not only of set-theoretic music in the mold of Babbitt, but also of the serial experiments of Schönberg and his school, that the intellectual order imposed on the music by the composer is not the order that we hear in it, when we hear it as music. It is an "encrypted" order, which is there for the expert, but that requires no *musical* experience for its decoding.

The defiance of the audience has extended from composer to performer. Indeed, the listening culture has been far more seriously damaged in recent years by the fossilization of performance than it has by the antibourgeois snobbery of the avant-garde. The cult of authentic performance has placed an ever thickening barrier between modern audiences and the classical tradition, so that they are now as much cut off from the past of our musical culture as they are from its present. A healthy musical culture is a culture of arrangements, transcriptions, and variations, in which the great works of the past are brought into living relation with modern ears.

We should not ask: what sounds did Bach intend? For he was writing for an audience whose ears had not encountered the strains of romantic harmony, and who did not seek, in music, for a refuge from the din of modern life. We should ask, instead, what *would* Bach have wanted if he were living now? Would he have wanted his music to be played on authentic instruments, with baroque ornamentation, by musicians for whom this whole attempt is an exercise in scholarship? Or would he have wished us rather to finger out his fugues on a Steinway grand, and so bring them into relation with the great tradition of his successors?

In a living culture, the dead are still present among the living. But when a culture dies it is ceremonially buried in a museum. This burial has now been set in motion by the movement that insists on calling Buxtehude, Gibbons, Purcell, and Bach "early music," and subjecting them to special sanitized treatment, as though they must be touched with rubber gloves until finally mummified. This movement arose alongside musical modernism, and is complementary to it, being a reaction against the vulgarity and excess of popular taste. Like the avant-garde, it is an attempt to wrest music from its adherents, and to reserve it for the experts.

The first step was to produce a "historical musicology" by squeezing music into the card index that Jacob Burckhardt and Heinrich Wölfflin had devised for the history of art. Henceforth, Bach was to be known as a baroque composer, just as Wren was a baroque architect, Rubens a baroque painter, and Milton a baroque poet. A concept invented by Burckhardt and Wölfflin in order to make a fine but important distinction between styles of architecture was elevated into a spiritual category, a *Zeitgeist*, and tied immovably to the chronology of Western culture. The effect of this label has been to imprison Bach's soul in the period that gave birth to his body, and to consign his music to a glass case in the museum of culture. The message is that we are no longer to enjoy this music, except through the filter of scholarship that will relieve us of its smell.

This scholarly approach is revealed in the very names of "authentic" performers: London Baroque Ensemble, Concentus Musicus, Musica Antiqua Köln, The Parley of Instruments, Collegium Aureum, the Consort of Musicke, the Orchestra of the Age of the Enlightenment, or such twee extravagances as Les Arts Florissants and La Grande Ecurie et la Chambre du Roi—a title worthy of Molière's *Précieuses ridicules*. The tired feeling that so many "authentic" performances induce can be compared to the atmosphere of a modern museum. A painting receives its final tribute from the scholar only in the form of a catalogue entry. Hence it is assumed that the proper place for a painting—even a minor painting—is not on the wall of a private house, where it can bestow joy and dignity on the life surrounding it, but in the gallery of some great museum, to be gaped at by weary multitudes as they wander from picture to picture in a state of well-informed fatigue. Likewise the works of the "early" or "ancient" composers have been confiscated by scholarship. They no longer have a place in our homes, played on our own familiar instruments, but are arranged behind the glass of authenticity, staring bleakly from the other side of an impassable screen.

The "authentic" performer, using "authentic" instruments, is imitating someone long since dead, and acting from aesthetic motives that were unavailable to his vanished predecessor. We might enjoy the result, but not as the original audience enjoyed the original performance. For the music is now presented to us under the aspect of its "pastness," and enjoyed partly on that account. In an essay titled "The Musicologist and the Performer," the critic Richard Taruskin put the point another way:

> Even at their best and most successful, or especially at their best and most successful, historical reconstructionist performances are in no sense recreations of the past. They are quintessentially modern performances, modernist performances in fact, the product of an aesthetic wholly of our own era, no less time-bound than the performance styles they would supplant.

The reference to modernism is exact. For the authentic performance arises from a consciousness of the past that is available only to those who feel themselves irremediably sundered from it. It expresses an *anthropologist's* view of our musical culture, a view from outside, meticulous in its search for curious details, but sharing only distantly in the inward compulsion, the belief in itself, from which the culture grew. It therefore includes the same tacit reprimand of the ordinary musical ear that was delivered by the modernists. We now find ourselves surrounded by performers and composers who distance themselves from their musical inheritance, and who look with disdain on those who are still immersed in it as having no sense of the distinction between a cliché and an authentic gesture.

The most curious thing in all this is that both the avant-garde and the authentic performers, who began life as defiant nonconformists standing against the mass of musical mankind, have become the new establishment. It is they who receive the government grants, the international prizes, the accolades in the press, and the scholarly treatises devoted to their work. In Britain it is unheard of for a music critic to say of Harrison Birtwistle that his music is as factitious as it sounds, or that the work of some tonal composer like Robin Holloway or David Matthews ought to be rewarded as Birtwistle is rewarded, with subsidized performances all over the globe. And it is almost impossible now to attend a rousing performance of the *Messiah* in Mozart's version, with massed choirs and full symphony orchestra, notwithstanding the popularity that would certainly attend such an event. All performances of "early" music—which, by convention, means any music before Haydn and Mozart—are heavily censored both by those who sponsor them and by those who review then. Only in the privacy of your own home would you dare now to play the Bach violin concertos with the full vibrato and portamento that they need, and that have been publicly banned.

The retreat into "authentic" performance, and the rise of the modernist avant-garde, justified themselves as reactions against the depravity of popular taste. The public ear, it was said, had become so habituated to the devices of tonal music, and so dulled by over-lush performances, that a complete break was necessary, lest the distinction between good and bad taste be forgotten. Here is what Schönberg has to say, in *Harmonielehre*, about the diminished seventh chord—the chord that does such sterling work in Mozart and Weber, and which is still in the back of Wagner's mind as he explores the seventh chords of his later harmony:

> This uncommon, restless, undependable guest, here today, gone tomorrow, settled down, became a citizen, was retired a philistine. The chord had lost the appeal of novelty, hence it had lost its sharpness, but also its luster. It had nothing more to say in a new era. Thus it fell from the higher sphere of art music to the lower music for entertainment. There it remains, as a sentimental expression of sentimental concerns. It became banal and effeminate. Became banal! It was not so originally. It was sharp and dazzling. Today, though, it is scarcely used any more except in that mawkish stuff (*Schmachtliteratur*) that later always apes what was, in great art, the important event.

This is the judgment with which Western music has subsequently had to contend: the judgment that the once sublime effects of tonal music had "become banal," largely as a result of their over-exploitation by the *Gebrauchsmusik* of the market place. Henceforth, there must be a radical divide between "art music," which is to be listened to, and the "lower music for entertainment" that is to be merely overheard. Those composers who continue to use the language of tonality in order to reach the ears and the hearts of ordinary concertgoers, were angrily dismissed by the avant-garde as traitors to the sacred cause of music. It soon became a sine qua non of musical sincerity that the composer should write music that was inaccessible to the tonal ear. People had to *graduate* to the new music, by learning to hear it in a more erudite way.

Behind all such ideas we feel the groundswell of a new and growing force: the force of popular music, which had broken free of the classical tradition and jettisoned the laws of taste. It strikes us now as amazing that *The Magic Flute* was once a paradigm of popular music. It is no less amazing that the dance music of the Strauss family—in which the principles of harmony, counterpoint, and voice-leading are meticulously obeyed, with themes and motifs subject to intricate symphonic development—should have had the place in ordinary lives that is now filled by hip-hop, grunge, and heavy metal. At some point, however, the popular and the classical began to diverge, and it is an awareness of this, rather than any dissatisfaction with the tonal tradition, that motivated the censorious theories and experiments of the modernists. Bartók, Enescu, Cecil Sharp, and Grainger were similarly inspired in their search for the "authentic" folk traditions, conscious that the language of popular music had become debased, and that the devices borrowed so freely from the classical tradition were threatening to extinguish the still small voice of natural human society.

Although Schönberg first made the suggestion, it was his disciple Theodor Adorno who exalted the antagonism between serious and popular music into the central drama of our musical culture. For Adorno, popular music had, by borrowing the devices of tonality, also polluted them beyond redemption. Henceforth, these devices must be avoided, since any use of them would result in sentimental cliché. Popular music was part of the "false consciousness" of capitalist society, a means to reconcile the masses to their condition by coating it in sugar. Only the music of the avant-garde could free itself from the ideological miasma that had poisoned the realm of tonality.

63

Adorno was not referring to R.E.M., U2, or AC/DC. He was dismissing the melodious and sophisticated music of our parents and grandparents: Gershwin, Cole Porter, Rodgers and Hammerstein, Louis Armstrong, Glenn Miller, and Ella Fitzgerald. This blanket condemnation did nothing to shore up the crumbling barriers of taste. For those things condemned by Adorno are better than anything that hits the charts today; by dismissing them as unfit for judgment, Adorno encouraged the belief that, outside the tradition of "art" music, anything goes.

At the same time, Adorno's intransigence raises in its most acute form the question whether our musical culture will survive. It can survive only if music has a place in our lives as an object of enjoyment and communication. If all that remains to us besides pop are sterilized performances of the classics, in which scholarship prevails over taste, or nightmarish "sound effects" from the modernist laboratory, then the tradition of "art" music is dead. Yet it was not dead when Adorno wrote his diatribes. Music still had a place in people's lives outside the concert hall. People sang and played the popular songs of the day, arranged them for jazz combo and marching band, incorporated them in their free improvisations at home and in church. The custom of hymn-singing persisted, and provided to the musical ear an easy and faultless education in the rules of four-part harmony. Tonality was a familiar daily companion, and it is this, more than any injection of scholarship, that created the musically literate audiences that abounded in our cities. It is precisely the music that Adorno despised which opened the ears of the general public to the classical masterpieces. And it is the loss of this repertoire of half-serious music, through which the language of tonality was effortlessly internalized, that has led to the eclipse of listening.

Again: the crisis of our musical culture does not, in my view, stem from the collapse of tonality. It stems from the quite peculiar condition in which music has been put by this loss of its half-serious variety, and by the consequent disappearance of the judgment of taste from ordinary listening. The sundering of "highbrow" from "lowbrow," "classical" from "popular," has left a gap between the language of serious music and the ears of the young—a gap that was once filled with hymns, carols, and Broadway musicals, but which is now empty except for the works of Sir Andrew Lloyd Webber, whose popularity, however, is a continuing reminder of the musical starvation in which most people live. This no man's land between high and popular culture was vacated only recently, and the atonal modernists must take much of the blame. Debussy bequeathed his harmonies to jazz, and jazz its rhythms to Stravinsky. Gershwin, Milhaud, Constant Lambert, and Bernstein wrote music that is neither highbrow nor lowbrow, while even the Broadway musical is grounded in harmony and counterpoint. The long tradition of musical utterance, which enabled our parents to hum with equal facility an aria by Mozart or a melody by Nat "King" Cole, was a precious icon of humanity. You can hear its echoes still in The Beatles or Buddy Holly, and to sing or move to this music is to take one step across the divide between popular and classical culture. You are beginning to think and feel *musically*—with an awareness of the voice not as a sound only, but as an expression of the soul.

The loss of the half-serious in music has led to a popular music devoid of taste, in which beat is the unifying force, and harmony and melody have atrophied. The dependence on beat has produced a new kind of audience, an audience that moves to music in a way that was traditionally forbidden by the culture of listening. Lacking all but the most rudimentary experience of melody and harmony, this audience has been effectively cut off from the classical tradition. Young people are frankly puzzled by the sight of adults listening in a concert hall to complex sounds that have no percussive "back-up," and which move through elaborate excursions that are seldom if ever repeated. From their perspective, this whole practice makes sense only on the assumption that something erudite and scholarly is taking place, and that the sounds of the orchestra are not enjoyed but *studied*. The pop fan joins with the modernist in accepting the absolute dichotomy between highbrow and lowbrow music.

Pop music, however, has no survival value—less even than the music-hall songs that are disinterred from time to time and heard with such helpless nostalgia. Although it wears away the ears of those who live with it, pop cannot provide the basis for a true musical culture. It has no capacity for allusion, development, or cross-reference, no ability to free itself from the mechanical devices that are the principal source of its musical appeal. It will always be a sterile and life-negating force, from which nothing proceeds apart from a habit of distraction. Eventually, like television, it will either lose its adherents, or reduce them to a zombielike condition that will isolate them from the past of mankind. In such conditions, a new culture of listening will begin to emerge.

We are already seeing this happen. The avant-garde persists now only as a state-funded priesthood ministering to a dying congregation. We have seen the demotion of serialism from the obligatory language of modern music to a stylistic eccentricity in free competition with the tonal styles; we have witnessed, too, the renunciation of experiment for experiment's sake and the attempt to integrate the modernist discoveries into a *lingua franca* that will be not so much posttonal as pantonal. Atonal music proved unable either to find an audience or to create one. Its harsh interdictions and censorious theories threatened the musical culture by disparaging the natural bourgeois life on which it depends. They have ended up on the dustheap of history, to become an environmental hazard only when stirred by curious scholars.

The new audience does not feel the force of modernism's bleak imperatives. It is as yet a fragile audience: its ears muddied by pop music, and barely aware of the distinction between rhythm and beat. Yet it has encountered the old musical culture, and been inspired by it. We should not be surprised if this new audience prefers easy homophony to complex polyphony, endless repetition to continuous development, block chords to voiced harmonies, regular beat to shifting accent, and boundless chant to bounded melody. For such are the expectations fostered by popular culture. Nor should we be surprised if the new audience is animated by a religious longing, while being unable to distinguish the religious from the religiose, content with a sentimental image of a faith that, in its real version, stands too severely in judgment over the postmodern world view.

Indeed, it is only with the emergence of this "discultured" audience that Schönberg's vision of the final degeneracy of tonal music has been realized. Ears schooled in pop seek for beat instead of rhythm, for "backing" rather than voice-led harmony, and tunes that divide into croonable phrases. Such ears are initially deaf to counterpoint, and to the real experience of tonality, as a working out in three dimensions of structural relationships. They hear in

Steve Reich or Philip Glass a kind of elevated and mesmerizing version of their favorite chords, and—having no sense of structure apart from repetition—imagine this to be a paradigm of serious music. In fact the music of the minimalists is far more banal and cliché-ridden than any of the half-serious music that has gone out of circulation. Its inability to pass from accompanying figures to polyphonic order expresses its helpless fixation with the chord, as opposed to the voices that fortify the chords as they move through on their melodic journeys.

The new audience also finds in the morose spirituality of Górecki an accessible experience of the "higher" life of music. For his is serious music, with a promise of release from the alienated world of popular culture. At the same time, it is composed as pop is composed, with monodic chanting over unvoiced chords. It is as though serious music must begin again, from the first hesitant steps of tonality, in order to capture the postmodern ear.

This is not to disparage the discultured audience. There is no doubt that, thanks to composers like Górecki and Tavener, the bourgeois ear is again being opened to music. Nevertheless, the thinness of this new music reminds us of the great task that lies before the art of sound: the task of recovering tonality as the imagined space of music, and of restoring the spiritual meaning with which that space was filled. I doubt that this act of restoration can be accomplished in Tavener's or Górecki's way: a musical equivalent of *Four Quartets* is needed—a rediscovery of the tonal language, which will also redeem the time. Many of our contemporaries have aimed at this—Nicholas Maw, John Adams, Robin Holloway, and Alfred Schnittke. But none, I think, has yet succeeded.

November 1996

Knocking about the Ruins

John Gross

THE only amusing thing I ever heard Hannah Arendt
say—admittedly I only met her once or twice—was at
a seminar in Princeton. The speaker was Dwight Mac-
donald; his subject was the inanity (or worse) of popular
culture, and as he warmed to his theme, the counterexample he increasingly invoked was that of Europe. On the
one hand Masscult and Midcult; on the other hand Athens,
Florence, Paris, Weimar . . . He drifted on in this vein for
about five minutes, until Arendt, who was sitting in the
front row, permitted herself a very audible whisper: "Ach,
Dwight, I could tell you a thing or two about that old
Europe of yours."

No one in his right mind would want to defend the
European past *en bloc*. In the twentieth century, Europe's
gifts to the world have included Nazism and Communism,
and even before that Europeans had quite as much to be
ashamed of in their history as Asians, Africans, or anyone
else. No, if one worries about the future of the European
past, it is as well to make clear that the term is being used
in a highly selective manner. It is shorthand, first, for the
positive achievements of European culture, and, secondly,
for the principle of social continuity—not stasis or blind
resistance to change, but continuity.

In speaking of European culture, one immediately runs

into an age-old problem. How far, except at a fairly high level of abstraction, does it actually exist? If you search long enough in the corridors of Brussels, you can no doubt discover a few officials who regard themselves as essentially European, and only incidentally French, German, or whatever; but the vast majority of Europeans continue to think of themselves first as French, German, or whatever. Europe remains a collection of cultures—interlinked, sometimes overlapping, but still distinct; and the same is even truer of the various historical legacies which European groups do or don't share. The past that a Russian brings to bear on his experience is as different from that of an Italian as that of a Norwegian is from that of an Irishman, or that of a Portuguese from that of a Pole.

Perhaps this will slowly change as economic and political integration proceeds. It certainly hasn't changed yet. On the other hand, some traditional boundaries *have* become blurred: the past twenty or thirty years have seen an unprecedented drawing together of European habits and attitudes, especially among the young, and there are times when one feels that one really is witnessing the emergence of a trans-European culture. But it is a phenomenon that has little to do with the institutions of the European Union, still less to do with immemorial traditions— *l'Europe aux anciens parapets*—and everything to do with prosperity, fashion, easy travel, and the mass media.

Many of the ingredients of the common brew will be tediously familiar to Americans; most of them, indeed, are American in origin. Rock, rap, Rollerblades; Disney and McDonald's; Quentin Tarantino, Beavis and Butt-head, Michael Jackson; and, if you want a handy symbol to sum up the whole phenomenon, you couldn't do much better, for the moment, than the ubiquitous baseball cap. There was a comic strip running in the London *Spectator*, about an obstreperous youth called Henry King, which gave some idea of how acute this last problem has become: the only real happiness Henry's parents know is when they are put in touch with a surgeon who has pioneered an operation designed to remove baseball caps from teenagers' heads. Not that the fashion is confined to adolescents. Princess Diana is a great wearer of baseball caps. So was the late Robert Maxwell.

There is, of course, nothing new about the enormous impact of American popular culture in Europe. It is a story as old as Hollywood and Tin Pan Alley; as old as Phineas T. Barnum (and in some respects, let it be said, a tribute to the superior energy and efficiency of the American product). But two things have changed over the past generation or so. First, Europeans have become more adept at generating mass entertainment and catering for mass consumption, in a manner which may still ultimately derive from American models but is far from merely imitative. (The Beatles were an obvious landmark here.) Secondly, pop culture is now so pervasive that it is thought of as being international rather than primarily American. There is much less transatlantic glamour attaching to it than there once was. It is part of the air that everybody breathes.

It has also had the effect, as it has gathered power, of making the past seem not merely old, but obsolete. What inducement is there, in a world of instant gratification and continual change, for thinking about the past at all? Consider the lyrics of today's pop songs: for the most part their range of reference is as narrow and impoverished as their vocabulary. The world began yesterday. But it wasn't always like that. In the early years of the century, the British musi-

cal-hall star Marie Lloyd used to sing a song that went,
"I'm one of the ruins that Cromwell knocked about a bit":
it was one of her greatest hits, and we can assume that her
largely working-class audience had at least some idea who
Cromwell was. Today Britain must spend at least fifty times
as much on education as it did in Marie Lloyd's time—and
if you came across a reference to Cromwell in a current pop
song, it would seem as out of place as a Greek hexameter.

Even the strongest cultural traditions have been eroded
by the new dispensation. Italy is the land of opera, and one
of the happiest features of the Italian love of opera is that it
has deep popular roots. But for anyone inclined to take too
rosy a view of the situation, a poll of 1,500 Italians recently
published in the *Corriere della Sera* makes instructive
reading. Over half of those questioned, given a choice of
composers, thought that Verdi's *Aïda* was by Beethoven;
on the other hand most of them had no difficulty identifying the soundtrack of *Pulp Fiction*. Asked who, in their
opinion, best represented Italian music abroad, they voted
for a number of local pop stars in preference to what might
have seemed the predictable choice of Pavarotti.

Complaints about the decline of "cultural literacy" must
be almost as common in Europe as they are in America. In
every part of Europe, I would guess—but I will confine
myself to Britain, the only country of which I can speak
with anything like assurance.

Every so often, British newspapers carry shock-horror
stories about children's lack of general knowledge. Teachers—some teachers—recount the latest examples of their
students' ignorance with gloomy relish. But has there actually been a deterioration in this respect? Weren't things,
as many people claim, just as bad in the past—a past which
we have either forgotten or idealized?

It will probably never be possible to provide conclusive proof one way or the other, but certainly there is no shortage of evidence pointing to a decline. A recent instance, widely remarked on, is the return, after a number of years' absence, of a popular television program called *University Challenge*, a general-knowledge quiz in which teams from different colleges are pitted against one another. In the 1960s and 1970s, the questions were difficult and the scores impressively high. In the 1990s, the questions remain difficult and most of the scores are depressingly low. They would be lower still if they weren't buoyed up by lots of marks scored for questions about rock music, a category which was barely acknowledged twenty or twenty-five years ago. Here, at least, the students display solid scholarship — almost, you might say, to the point of pedantry.

An even clearer demonstration of declining standards was provided this year by a Gallup survey in which two groups of people, one consisting of over-forty-fives and the other of under-twenty-fives, were asked a series of rudimentary questions about British history — Guy Fawkes, Sir Christopher Wren, 1066 and all that. The gulf between the old (or middle-aged) and the young was even plainer than one might have expected. The first group chalked up respectable scores, while the second group floundered. Most of the over-forty-fives, for instance, knew that the monarch in whose reign the Spanish Armada was defeated was Elizabeth. For most of the under-twenty-fives, it was a mystery.

It isn't only a question of information, however, but also one of values, interests, and attitudes. Every year, for example, Madame Tussaud's waxworks museum hands out a questionnaire asking visitors who they think is the greatest figure, past or present, British or foreign, on display. In 1960, the year in which the poll was instituted, the largest number of votes went to Churchill—a somewhat time-bound and parochial choice, perhaps, but hardly a discreditable one. This year the winner was Superman, with Princess Diana as runner-up.

But why should most people be expected to know any better, when one considers the influences by which they are bombarded? The gods of the media have become more real than reality—if a public figure has ever been portrayed in a play or film, for instance, his obituary is more likely to be accompanied by a picture of the actor who played him than by a picture of the man himself; and not a day goes by without a fresh assault being launched on established manners and habits of thought.

So much of the change is gratuitous, too, its only real purpose being to demonstrate that a marketing director, an editor, a producer knows how to stir things up. A particularly galling example is the current fashion for renaming pubs. Few British institutions, one might have supposed, were more indestructible, more part of the landscape, than the Red Lion, the Rose and Crown, the Wheatsheaf, or the King's Head. Now you are liable to wake up and find that their names have been replaced overnight by something facetious and disagreeable—the Slug and Lettuce, say, or the Rat and Parrot—with a glossy new signboard to match. There is a pub in Kent that is mentioned in Dickens (though it is much older than that) which until the other day was always known as the Guy, Earl of Warwick. Now it is the Ferret and Trouser Leg. Not a major tragedy, perhaps, but another thread torn from the social fabric. The Red Lion and the Rose and Crown have something in common, however tenuous, with the Tabard in Chaucer or the Boar's Head in Shakespeare. The Ferret and Trouser Leg is a publicist's bad joke.

What is particularly disheartening about the junking of the past is how little resistance has been offered by institutions which not so long ago would have been considered bulwarks of social stability. On the contrary, many of them seem anxious to speed the process on its way: the sentries have abandoned their posts and clambered aboard the bandwagon. Take the Church of England. For anyone with a sense of its history, and of the cultural coloration which it has always given to English life as a whole, it is impossible not to feel dismayed by its attempts to jazz itself up and project a user-friendly image. One especially striking aspect of decline, which impoverishes everybody, is its attitude to language and liturgy. For the past thirty-five years, ever since the publication of the New English Bible, it has been busy turning poetry into prose, and pretty undistinguished prose at that; and though its efforts in this respect have met with plenty of criticism, it continues to press blithely ahead. A new Church of England songbook, aimed primarily at children, but also intended for adults "who want to let their hair down," includes compositions bearing such titles as *I Like Eating Sandwiches and Cakes* and *Prayer Is Like a Telephone*. In one song, *Who's the King of the Jungle?*, the congregation is invited to act and sound like monkeys. Another contains the line "He gives me lips to eat my chips." One hopes the children are going to enjoy all this stuff; but reading about it, I couldn't help recalling D. H. Lawrence's beautiful essay "Hymns in a Man's Life," with its tribute to the power of hymns—good hymns, the kind that are being driven out by cake and sandwiches—to seize and enlarge a child's imagination.

One of the Church's latest stunts has been to unveil a

corporate logo (who would ever have supposed that it needed one?) which has been specially devised for it by a commercial design group: an emblem combining the letter *c*, the letter *e*, and a cross, to be displayed on notepaper, signboards, and so forth in "warm episcopal purple." The purpose, we are told, is to improve the Church's credibility and to make it "more relevant to younger people." In this sign shalt thou conquer.

Then there is the BBC. The old BBC had its faults (as what does not?), but it also had enormous virtues. Many of those virtues still survive, in depleted or fragmented fashion: if you listened and viewed selectively enough, you might just about persuade yourself the character of the Corporation was essentially unchanged. But it would be an illusion. Over the past generation a great deal of the BBC's regular output has been coarsened, or radicalized, or both. Soap operas about the supposedly everyday life of sup- posedly ordinary people now feature incest, AIDS, cocaine, and gangland killings in pell-mell profusion. (Their pred- ecessors look positively pastoral by contrast.) The most popular current broadcaster on BBC radio, someone called Chris Evans, is a hooligan who has to be heard to be believed. On magazine programs and the like, middle-class values are constantly assailed and ridiculed. At least, middle-class values are what they tend to get called: in my experience they have always been shared by most working- class people as well, but "middle-class" has established itself as a reliable term of abuse.

One further example of shifting standards—a smaller one, but highly symptomatic. The National Portrait Gallery in London is a noble institution, possibly the finest gallery of its kind in the world. Until some fifteen years ago, in ac- cordance with its Victorian statutes, it wasn't allowed to purchase or accept portraits of living men and women. That almost inevitably had to change; and given that the Gallery is already well supplied with the dead, it is no great surprise if the living now make up around half the annual list of acquisitions. What would have been almost impossible to predict, on the other hand, even fifteen years ago, is the composition of the latest such list. Businessmen (of the headline-catching variety) and entertainers are generously represented, science and scholarship barely at all. There are no classical musicians, but space has been found for the pop singer Sting and for Malcolm McLaren, the founder of the punk group the Sex Pistols.

This democratization (shall we call it?) has been going on for some time. Step into the twentieth-century section of the Gallery, and where the first face that caught your eye might once have been that of Vaughan Williams or John Maynard Keynes, you are liable to find yourself confronted by sports stars, fashion designers, television personalities. The Gallery's portrait of Auden now hangs alongside a particularly glitzy portrait of the pop singer Elton John, in a room dominated by a large picture of Paul McCartney. And meanwhile notable figures from the past have been relegated or removed. Mrs. Gaskell, for example, has been packed off to a branch of the Gallery in Wales.

There is no need, perhaps, to cite further instances of the way in which new values have taken hold in old places. To do so might seem to be laboring the point. Yet part of the point is the sheer number of such instances. They keep streaming in, day after day, from all directions. A famous school, Harrow—Churchill's old school, and Byron's—builds its own theater: the first play the pupils perform in it is *Angels in America*. The Post Office turns down requests for a commemorative stamp marking the centenary of William Morris in favor of a stamp celebrating a television puppet of the 1950s called Muffin the Mule. It isn't some eager new university but a Cambridge college that elects Emma Thompson an honorary fellow. It isn't some fly-by-night publisher but Faber and Faber that gives a rock guitarist a place on the editorial board.

The most effective remedy for our cultural discontents is naturally education—or it would be, if one didn't know better. Never has it been more up to teachers to defend high culture and protect what is worth preserving from the past. Never have so many of them gloried in not doing so.

The situation, one must concede, is complicated. Consider the academic study of history. Readers of *The New Criterion* don't need to be told about the troubles that beset it in America, and similar problems are far from unknown in England. Neo-Marxists toil in their vineyards, Michel Foucault casts a long shadow, radical feminists go about their appointed tasks. But there are powerful countervailing forces as well. History remains a flourishing discipline in Britain: to take only one example, last year saw the publication of a remarkable history of Europe, which would have done credit to any age, by the British historian Norman Davies. As long as such books appear, it would be absurd to launch into a wholesale jeremiad.

Publicity can be misleading, too. Penguin Books is bringing out a multivolume history of Britain, to replace the one which they published in the years following World War II (and which has been a standby for students ever since). In his initial announcement, the general editor, David Cannadine, made it sound as though it was going to be ruthlessly revisionist, cutting Britain down to size, written from the perspective of a small island rather than that of a former power with global pretensions. This is quite a popular line at present. It suits the national mood of masochism; one suspects that it also plays rather well in America. In reality, one need hardly add, no serious British historian has been in danger of writing triumphalist or imperialist history for a very long time. So one gritted one's teeth and waited. But the first two volumes of the project —on the seventeenth century and the twentieth century— have now appeared, and they turn out to be solid, straightforward, and quite free from any taint of trendiness.

Professional historians must be left to fight their battles among themselves. More important, for society as a whole, is the teaching of history in schools, and the general hum and buzz of historical awareness in the world at large. Here—witness the Gallup survey, witness those television quizzes—there is undoubted cause for gloom. The history taught in British state schools is now mostly confined to recent times. In foreign affairs, it tends to be history of the we-were-wrong variety; in domestic affairs, it puts disproportionate emphasis on "history from below." It attaches greater value to empathy than to facts: children are supposed to explore and find out for themselves (with a few nudges toward the Left). A British newspaper, commenting on the number of younger respondents to the Gallup survey who didn't know about the Armada, suggested that there were only two possibilities: either they hadn't been taught about it at all, or they had simply been told that there had been an Anglo-Spanish naval engagement, and then asked to write an essay expressing the feelings of the widow of a Spanish sailor.

There may be worse to come. The crisis in history-teaching is part of a more general breakdown of standards in education; it is all of a piece with the policy of dismissing instruction in punctuation and grammar as "hegemonic," or the belief that you empower children by not correcting their mistakes. But history has also been specifically targeted. There have been proposals for removing it from the school syllabus altogether; and if that sounds far-fetched, consider the recent experience of Spain. There is at present no teaching of history in Spanish schools, although the government is planning to reinstate it as soon as possible: it was abolished by the previous government, led by the Socialist Felipe González, and replaced by a cooked-up course (for students between the ages twelve and sixteen) labeled "social sciences." According to the new Spanish minister for education and culture, Esperanza Aguirre, it wasn't until she began examining the situation in detail that its full bleakness was brought home to her—that she realized that there was now no reason why a Spanish schoolchild should ever learn of the existence of Julius Caesar, for example. (It is somewhat droll, given the revelations about British ignorance of the Armada, that another figure she should cite—but she was speaking to a British journalist, so perhaps she was teasing—was Sir Francis Drake: "A Spanish child has a right to learn about Drake. And about the galleons he looted.")

As for the positive content of the social sciences course, it turns out, according to Señora Aguirre, to be even more slanted than one might have supposed. The textbooks prepared for it are littered with references to neo-colonialism and "the crisis in the liberal-bourgeois world." A section on "the evolution of ideology after the Second World War" contains expositions of Marxism and existentialism, but capitalism is mentioned only in connection with such topics as Third World debt.

It seems to me unlikely (though you can never be sure) that the Spanish experiment will be attempted in Britain, and if it were, I doubt whether it would have the effect its architects intended. The chief effect of dismantling old-style education, as far as I can make out, has not been to create an appetite for new-style education, but to create an even bigger vacuum for "youth culture" to rush in and fill. A student who has been force-fed Marxism and existentialism is more likely than ever, once he escapes, to take refuge in the excitements of rock and pop (and possibly even stronger substances).

The manufacturers of popular entertainment still show a certain fitful interest in the past, but much less of one than formerly; and one isn't necessarily inclined to feel grateful to them when they do. If I may intrude a personal note, I recently went back, for the first time for over thirty years, to take a look at the house where I spent my early childhood: it is now a video store, and the window was dominated by a life-size cut-out of Kevin Costner as Robin Hood. (Costner may well be an even bigger star in Europe than in America: "Kevin" is currently the most popular boy's name in France.) A lowering experience—though no doubt we can survive a politically correct version of Robin Hood, just as we can survive the hostile caricatures of British officials in the latest Disney version of *The Jungle Book*. The distortions and anti-English bias of a Hollywood movie like *Braveheart* (about the Scottish hero William Wallace) are more serious, however, and those of a movie like *Michael Collins* positively pernicious. It shouldn't be forgotten, in fact, that the future of the European past is partly being shaped in America. And when it comes to education proper, and the recent decision that New York school-children should be taught that the Irish famine of the 1840s was on a par with the Holocaust, what can we do but throw up our hands? (One place where this decision has excited interest, not surprisingly, is Germany, and it is a sign of the way media culture tends to work, even in the most distinguished quarters, that the *Frankfurter Allgemeine Zeitung* should have commissioned an article about it, not from one of the many excellent Irish or English historians who would have been available, but from the literary critic and republican sympathizer Terry Eagleton.)

Meanwhile, there is still a lively public interest in history, and in many respects it is still very well catered for. Every week, for example, large numbers of people visit the historic homes administered by the National Trust (though they don't always win the approval of their intellectual betters for doing so: Jonathan Miller, with his inimitable command of metaphor, has said that the British would "walk through a lake of pus" in order to see a country house). Again, serious historical exhibitions are still packed and serious historical biographies still figure prominently on publishers' lists: a leading daily paper can still run a series extending over several weeks on the latest state of knowledge about Roman Britain. And there are still serious historical programs on television, if you know where to look for them—though they tend to be shown at unsociable hours, and you can't help feeling that they have an increasingly old-fashioned air. A better guide to the future is probably the history channel on British satellite television, in which "history" all too often turns out to be what would once have been called current affairs, with a strong dash of show business. As I write, for example, half the current week's schedule consists of biographical programs; the subjects are George Bush, Saddam Hussein, Sherlock

Holmes, Lord Mountbatten, Hillary Clinton, O.J. Simpson, Yitzak Rabin, Jules Verne, Audrey Hepburn, and Buffalo Bill. You wonder whether they will ever get round to the ruins that Cromwell knocked about a bit.

The same triumph of short-term memory can be widely observed in other areas—in the study of literature, for example. It isn't uncommon to read about such things as the recent case of the headmaster whose school was accused of neglecting serious literature, and who protested that, far from it, his pupils were actually studying the classics: "this year we're doing Shakespeare and Sylvia Plath." No educational reformer, as far as I know, has yet proposed that schools should drop the literature of the past completely, but as time goes by poor Shakespeare has more and more had to shoulder the burden of representing it all by himself—or at most with a little assistance from Jane Austen or Hardy. Nor is the situation very different in the lower reaches of the British university system. It is now possible to study English at college level and emerge ignorant of almost everything written before the twentieth century.

It is against this background that some critics have found consolation in the recent wave of movies and television series based on literary classics. For sterner spirits, even the best of these adaptations, though they plainly vary a great deal in merit, are irreparably marred by anachronisms and false notes: they represent a betrayal. There are two irreconcilable doctrines—either "something is better than nothing," or "nothing but the best will do"—and I must admit that, like many people, I find myself caught between them. Fortunately, however, this isn't a major problem. If you don't like the adaptations, the books themselves are still there, waiting to be read without benefit of a go-between.

In the theater, on the other hand, the question of interpretation is inescapable, and in recent years, while I have
been working as a drama critic, hardly a week has gone
by without my being forced to consider our relationship—
and responsibilities—to the art of the past. Some of the
productions of classics that I see are admirable (and they
include productions of minor classics that theatergoers
haven't had a chance to see for generations). Many of them,
however, are disfigured by the kind of gimmicks that go
by the flattering name of "concepts" among their admirers,
and quite a few are insulting travesties of the works which
they purport to present. Time after time, though I ought to
know better by now, I settle down hoping to see *King Lear*,
or *The Tempest*, or *Hamlet*, and find myself watching a Lear
who starts off (in Act One, Scene One) in a wheelchair,
playing silly games, or an Ariel who ends up spitting in
Prospero's face, or an Ophelia whose dress is stained with
menstrual blood—you know the kind of thing. And it isn't
only Shakespeare who suffers in this way. Lady Bracknell
turns up played by a drag queen; Congreve's *The Way of the
World* is acted out amid rubbish stuffed into black plastic
bags.

Even the most unlikely candidates are given a going-
over. The other day, for instance, I saw a production of
Mrs. Warren's Profession, which is one of Bernard Shaw's
earliest plays, and one of his better ones. It was a good
production, for the most part, but in case we should think
he lacked originality the director had brought the action
forward from the 1890s to the 1920s, and a hundred social
nuances were lost in the process.

Still, Shakespeare remains the prime victim of "innovations," and one disastrous production stays in my mind
in particular—partly because of the initial sympathy with

which I approached it, partly because of its subsequent reception. Since the advent of the National Theatre, and the establishment of a permanent base for the Royal Shakespeare Company in London, Shakespeare has seldom been produced in the West End, and when a Shaftesbury Avenue management decided to stage *Much Ado about Nothing* several years back, it was the first Shakespeare production on that celebrated theatrical thoroughfare for forty years. I found it hard not to feel well disposed toward it in advance; in addition, my hopes were colored by memories of a magnificent production of the same play with John Gielgud that I had seen in the West End when I was young. But alas, this time Benedick had a droopy little moustache, capered around like a slapstick comedian in a silent movie, and spoke with a thick Ulster accent which bore no relation to the way anyone else spoke. Beatrice was a slattern who made her first entrance stuffing her mouth with a banana. "Sigh No More, Ladies" was turned into a square dance, complete with gingham dresses and jeans. The subtleties of the play were wrecked. The poetry went out the window.

That the production received some enthusiastic reviews didn't altogether surprise me. What was dismaying, on the other hand, was that it rapidly became that comparatively rare thing in the contemporary theater, a hit with the young. Friends told me that it had aroused an enthusiasm for Shakespeare in their children which they had never hoped to see. After I had made some uncomplimentary remarks about it in the course of a talk, a woman in the audience came up to me with a stricken look: she was a schoolteacher who had taken her class to see it, and if I only knew what it was usually like trying to get young people interested . . . How could I fail to feel a twinge of sympathy? But whatever the young people were getting out of it, I don't think it was Shakespeare. There are times when something is less than nothing.

And what is the updating and relocating of plays that takes place in the theater all about? Occasionally, it serves a clear political purpose. Not long ago, for example, there was a big production of Euripides' *Trojan Women* at the National Theatre, in which the Trojans (good) were presented as an array of international types, while the Greeks (bad) were uniformed Americans straight from Vietnam. But this kind of direct equation is less common than it used to be. Most of the juggling of periods and styles (as in the *Much Ado*) is far more wanton and arbitrary. There is logic in a doublet-and-hose production of Shakespeare (which is about the most revolutionary thing anyone could propose at present), or in a production which reflects a play's setting (Romans wearing togas), or in a modern-dress production, but most contemporary productions are none of these things. Instead, they abound in strange juxtapositions. A duchess who might have stepped out of a Renaissance painting chain-smokes, while her brother is got up like a Ruritanian general. Russian boyars jostle with Edwardian clubmen and Italian *fascisti*. If half the Romans wear togas, the other half seem to be serving under Napoleon. Motorbikes appear from nowhere. Knights wear armor, when they are not sporting black leather, and humble folk shuffle along in what a colleague of mine calls "old overcoats." The preferred term in the trade for all this is "mixed period." The effect is a mishmash.

It may seem odd, given the semi-Marxist ideas that float around in the theater, that there aren't more attempts by directors to set Shakespeare in his social context. If there were, we would surely see more Elizabethan-dress productions. But perhaps the Marxism doesn't go very deep, and it would be truer to talk of a vague amorphous leftism. At all events, the impression we are left with by most modern productions of his work, and of other classics, is of the past as an impossible jumble. "'Tis all in pieces, all coherence gone."

A great deal of this reflects the desire to break things rather than the reality of breakage. Modern theater directors, like other modern artists and intellectuals (to say nothing of sub-artists and sub-intellectuals), are frequently engaged in selling an apocalyptic or anarchic version of the world which doesn't bear much relation to the way most people live—which probably doesn't bear much relation to the way most of them live themselves. Still, they find a widespread echo; and if they are part of the problem, that only means that the problem is even bigger than it would have been without them. We should do everything we can to resist the false diagnoses, the meretricious solutions, the revolutionary zeal of people who still haven't learned the lessons of the past eighty years; but in the end we are still liable to be left with the sensation of living in a society that is adrift, a society which has lost its narrative thread.

This is a condition which, however reluctantly, I believe we have got to learn to live with. We can work to defend what is left of our civic culture, and to restore some of what has been lost; but any panacea that is proposed for our disorders is likely to turn out to be much worse than the disease. I don't think we should underestimate the potential for tyranny that lurks in our society. Today's demagogue remains tomorrow's gauleiter. Today's ideologue remains tomorrow's commissar.

As for the future of the European past, it seems to me too big a question to admit of a coherent answer. The one thing we can safely predict about the past is that there is no going back to it. Beyond that, I think it probable that the culture of a federal Europe will grow steadily less European, in any traditional sense. There will be no shortage of festivals and galas and cultural commissions, but they will be synthetic, without roots. But I could be wrong, and meanwhile we can still learn from the past, and learn about it, and try to defend its achievements from the depredations of pop, postmodernism, and all the other forces ranged against them. There are endless battles to be fought, even if we lack a grand strategy.

December 1996

A Devitalized Wariness

Ferdinand Mount

WHENEVER we hear the word culture, we should reach for our scalpels. We will get nowhere if we fail to dissect, divide, discriminate: cultures, not culture. This is particularly true for Europeans. It may be plausible for Americans, inheritors of a continent and a culture which have remained united for two centuries, to think singular. But an inhabitant of any European nation is fooling himself if he talks about European culture as anything but irredeemably plural, an enormous pond muddied by closely related clumps of frogspawn. And if, in considering the condition of our culture, we sidle up to that related question, so alluring in its melancholy, of the death of the European past, then we must ask whose past, and which bits of it are dead or dying?

When people venture into these boggy regions, I think there are at least four distinct but overlapping kinds of loss or threatened loss that they would like to talk about. For convenience, I'll call them: first, the loss of knowledge, also known as the pursuit of ignorance or "dumbing down"; second, vulgarization; third, the loss of the past; and, fourth, the loss of national identity (there is a fifth loss which people don't talk about so much, but I shall say something about it). Unfortunately, most loss-mongers do not bother to distinguish between any of them. As a result, their jeremiads tend to be either ill-aimed or deploy excessive firepower for the target in question. I think that both British and American conservatives, though clearly right in some respects, are sometimes mistaken about the extent and nature of the damage. But I do not expect to make many converts on this particular battlefield, since for most combatants it is a question of first digging your trench and then staying in it, while firing continuously into the air. The best to be hoped for is that culture warriors may begin to get a glimmering that there are several different questions bundled up together here, and that they do not all deserve the same somber answer.

Books such as Allan Bloom's *The Closing of the American Mind* and J. H. Plumb's *The Death of the Past* have provoked, worried, and stimulated, but they have not always clarified. At times, Bloom, for example, simply rehearses the familiar lament that students these days are appallingly ignorant and obtuse, partly because "the old teachers who loved Shakespeare or Austen or Donne, and whose only reward for teaching was the perpetuation of their taste, have all but disappeared." At other times, the decadence he bemoans seems to be a specifically American disaster; you can become an American in a day, but it is an impoverished, etiolated sort of life you are letting yourself in for. At other times again, he follows Ortega y Gasset in identifying the entire modern world as flat, or narrow, or "built on low but solid ground" (Leo Strauss), wedded to mediocrity and deaf to the possibilities of transcendence. Thus, although the book is full of mordant asides and enchanting aphorisms, it is hard to tell whether what is wrong is primarily an educational problem that could be remedied by improving American schools, or an inferiority of national life and character that demands that the U.S.

should learn something from other cultures, or a human predicament which we all share in a post-Nietzschean world and which might take a little longer to put right.

We can at any rate start by tackling the simple question which first proposes itself (simple to identify, I mean, not to answer): the "dumbing down" question. Is the general, or average, or median level of education—and hence we may presume, of public discourse—being lowered, year by year, whether deliberately or accidentally?

It is easy enough to find examples from one's own experience where this is so. A nice, rarified instance: just before leaving Eton in 1957, I was taken to inspect the Latin and Greek verses which had been "sent up for good" (that is, shown to the Head Master) by Swinburne and one or two of his seventeen-year-old contemporaries at the school. There they were a century later, still tied together with Eton-blue ribbon. The handwriting was beautiful, the standard of versification infinitely higher than anything we could have managed with our mechanistic resort to stock epithets. All the same, we in the 1950s were still being set the same tasks as Swinburne and his contemporaries and embarking upon them at roughly the same age, in our early teens. Today, of course, few boys in Britain, and still fewer in the United States, attempt such versification at all. The classical culture automatically available to, say, the generation of Byron, Peel, and Aberdeen at Harrow School, and to their social inferiors at lesser schools all over the country, has vanished.

Is the same fate now beginning to overtake the broad body of historical knowledge—I mean, "modern history," that is, from the Middle Ages on—which was assumed to be the possession of any educated man? Such knowledge would comprise for an educated Englishman of any class between 1850 and 1950: on the military front, say, some idea of the Hundred Years War, the Wars of the Roses, the Civil War, and the Peninsular War; on the civil front, an understanding (usually of a whiggish sort) of the development of Parliament, the rise of social legislation, and the industrialization of the country. But now? Kenneth Baker, a former British education secretary, recently declared in a book review that "the teaching of history before 1900 is fast disappearing from our schools." Two examining boards have withdrawn GCSE exams (the main exam taken in British high schools), on the Tudors and Stuarts and on the Victorian age, because so few pupils were choosing these courses, preferring to opt for post-1900 and world history.

The reduced time left for history in the curriculum of most schools—certainly those attended by my children (now in their mid-twenties)—must have had some effect. After all, to have kept one's historical knowledge to the same approximate level would require a steady *increase* in the amount of time devoted to history. A person who, as well as the knowledge mentioned above, has not also some notion of the course and causes of both world wars and the rise and fall of Nazism and Communism is at least as uneducated as someone who has never read *Hamlet* or *Middlemarch*.

A recent Gallup poll showed that young people in particular are more familiar with the characters in TV soap operas than with the leading figures in British history. Seventy-four percent know that the landlady of the Queen Victoria pub in the Cockney saga "EastEnders" is the actress Barbara Windsor, but only 61 percent can identify the real Queen Victoria as Britain's longest serving monarch. I am surprised the score is as high as 61 percent. The fact, after all, is of no huge significance; an educated person might well think that the correct answer was Queen Elizabeth I, George III, or one of the longer-lived Plantagenets. I am more impressed by the fact that 89 percent of the sample, including 82 percent of sixteen- to twenty-four-year-olds, knew that it was Guy Fawkes who tried to blow up the Houses of Parliament in 1605—a fact of considerable significance for the subsequent course of British history and, as it happens, the subject of Mr. Baker's gloomy book review.

One defense to this charge-sheet rests precisely on the fact that these days there is much more to learn. A reasonably dutiful undergraduate today will probably know more chemistry than Goethe knew, more than Prince Rupert or even Robert Boyle did. This defense is far from negligible, though it has its flaws. Many sub-branches of the "modern sciences," after all, are bogus and usurp precious learning time; others don't belong in schools, but can be picked up later at the workplace, or in postgraduate study. Schools should teach more mathematics, less computer science; more history, less history of art; and so on. The modern syllabus does include more genuine topics than the trivium and quadrivium ever dreamed of: more geography, more genetics, more politics. Against that, a new British government inquiry has just shown that the A (for "advanced") level examinations for chemistry, mathematics, and English are easier than they were twenty years ago. Broader means shallower, as Kingsley Amis might have said.

Classical studies, which is enjoying a modest revival on British campuses, now involves a bunch of non-linguistic aspects of classical civilization: slavery, the position of women, legal history, trade flows, medicine, even cookery.

Softer options than Sapphics and Alcaics perhaps, but not wholly contemptible if the project is to gain some understanding of the period. The concept of "understanding" is certainly vulnerable to specious and sentimental techniques, notably the "empathizing" approach: "What would a Norman soldier have felt as his boat approached the shore of England in 1066?" All the same, while as keen as anyone to root out this kind of mushy history, I cannot bring myself to argue that what all this betokens is the death of the past in our minds. If anything, it is surely more a symptom of our minds softening, losing edge.

This calls for a pedagogic toughening up, a long march through the educational institutions certainly, but one led by hard-boiled teachers, not by fanatical *Kulturkämpfer*. True, some of the problems do spring from malign ideologies that have attempted to discredit, often with depressing ease, qualities previously thought essential to education, such as effort, competition, and accuracy; they have often managed to outlaw rote learning, written examinations, and other handy devices for fixing knowledge in one's head. Against these *sottises*, the counterattack has begun; it will need to be fierce and sustained. Yet one should add that the overcrowding of the curriculum also springs from the overeagerness of honest dolts. And even some of the most disastrous wrong turnings—in the teaching of reading, for example—were taken in the genuine belief that they really would help children to learn better.

Dumbing down is, I think, a reality, and it must be ferociously combatted, but it is not quite the same as vulgarization. There is, I agree, some spillover from the egalitarian fallacies in education to the loathing of high public culture which has pervaded the media. The flight from difficulty is common to both; so is the hostility to elitism. Yet even here there is a distinction to be drawn between what the levelers-down would like to do—namely, efface any distinction between high and low—and the far more important influence of popular taste bringing its own natural weight to bear.

Here we come to a popular-culture dilemma, which is at least as old as the invention of printing. Do you stay in business by giving the public what it wants, or do you give them what you think they ought to have? Caxton's early bestsellers were romances about kings and queens, collections of bawdy tales, and so on. Then as now, the popular market had to be served, for reasons of democracy no less than of commerce. When Sir Kenneth Clark took on the chairmanship in 1954 of the new commercial television authority in Britain, he stated, without any shame, that the *niveau* of the new station was to be that of the *Daily Mirror*—a saucy popular newspaper (these days twice as saucy). Neither he nor anyone else suggested that the new channel had any duty to civilization or any potential to aim higher: those who were opposed to ITV simply asserted that there should be no commercial television at all. Such opponents feared, not so much that commercial television would degrade the tastes of the masses, as that it would serve those preexisting tastes all too faithfully. And they were right.

The progressive vulgarizing of the British popular press —from the Victorian *Daily Telegraph*, to Northcliffe's *Daily Mail*, to Beaverbrook's *Daily Express*, to the old *Daily Mirror*, to Rupert Murdoch's *Sun*—can be seen as a kind of breaking through the upper and middle strata of seriousness and respectability to meet a vulgarity which was always lurking there, down at rock bottom. After all, you have to remember that the bestseller of 1528 was the tale of "How Howleglas set his hostess upon the hot ashes with her bare arse." If Hieronymous Bosch, why not Quentin Tarantino? If obscene puns are tolerable in Rabelais, or in Joyce, why not in the *Sun*? If T. S. Eliot, Proust, and Max Beerbohm all loved the music hall, why shouldn't we love soap operas?

To blame "commercial pressures" is a comfortable evasion. Pop culture *is* popular, likely to remain so, and cannot and should not be suppressed. Liberal democracy can muster no justification for stemming the flow of vulgarity, either by direct *diktat* or by indirect pressure. Democracy entails vulgarity, though it does not prescribe it. Dumbing down is a patronizing misunderstanding of democracy, but vulgarization is democracy's natural accompaniment.

In any case, vulgarization is not the same as the murder of the past. For vulgarization is no more hostile to the past than it is to the present; on the contrary, the vulgarizer responds with enthusiasm to cobwebs and crinolines and crusades. Hollywood cheapens, anachronizes, misshapes the past. But then it misshapes the present, and the future too, with the same innocent gusto. Hollywood has no more accurate notion of modern family life, say, than it has of the age of Louis XIV or ancient Rome.

By contrast, actual hatred of the past goes together with something quite different, with longing for a *tabula rasa*. Mao believed the Chinese to be "poor and blank"; that was what was so wonderful about them, because on a blank sheet of paper "the freshest and most beautiful characters can be written." Such yearnings to shake off the bonds of tradition, to make people over from scratch without any inherited sclerosis, that is a *political* project, one which is not at all the same as the dumbing-down process and will coincide with the latter only briefly, before moving in the opposite direction, that of interfering with and eventually suppressing popular tastes, as all effective dictatorships do —and must do—in their heyday. Hatred of the past is a disease of disenchanted intellectuals, not a consequence of vulgarization.

There is a milder variant of the revolutionary's outright hatred of the past, namely, the progressive's wish to be free of its shackles. Plumb, for example, as a good whig, ends his book with this blast:

> The old past is dying, its force weakening, and so it should. Indeed the historian should speed it on its way, for it was compounded of bigotry, of national vanity, of class domination. It was as absurd as that narrow Christian interpretation which Gibbon rightly scorned. May history step into its shoes, help to sustain man's confidence in his destiny, and create for us a new past as true, as exact, as we can make it, that will help us achieve our identity, not as Americans or Russians, Chinese or Britons, black or white, rich or poor, but as men.

There seems to be a contradiction lurking somewhere in there. If we are to be genuinely free of the past, why do we need historians? Conversely, the attempt to trace some kind of "ascent of man"—as Plumb says historians should— demands some degree of historicism; if it is a mountain or even a gentle gradient that over the centuries we have been climbing, the slope has to have existed before we did and our future must be partly determined by our past, so we cannot be free of it.

But, just as Keynes said that "practical men who believe

themselves to be free from any intellectual influences are usually the slaves of some defunct economist," so our enthrallment to our past does not depend upon our consciousness of it or upon any profound understanding of that past. A living culture is a dialogue between past and present but a dialogue in which one or the other may be unheard or indistinct, a Burkean contract but one that you may be unaware of having signed. Even in a religious context, the declaration, "Behold I make all things new," is more a cry for attention than a comprehensive truth. We discard parts of our past, take up others with fresh interest. This, after all, is what cultural historians show us doing ever since the last millennium, just as they show an appetite for vulgarity limited only by the unremitting censorship of the authorities.

For that reason, the vulgarization of the public media seems to me at worst harmless and at best a symptom of continuing resistance to dubious attempts to "improve" us. Those of us who wish to elevate public taste in the marketplace by, say, promoting the serious discussion of books would do better to suspend our lamentations now and then and set out to win more readers. We have to manage the feat which comes so hard to *enragés*, of keeping two ideas in one's head at the same time: that in a democracy people must not and cannot be prevented from taking their fun as they find it; but that, at the same time, we elevators of public taste have a duty to keep on offering the highest we can come up with, regardless of whether "they" love it when they see it.

It is certainly true that one field in which we wish to cultivate the highest—and here we move on to the next form of purported loss—is our own past. In this field, conservatives do have a specific crusade to wage; for here it is essential to insist, not only that culture largely consists in the accumulated deposit of the past and is impoverished if these deposits are neglected, but that we have a duty to pay particular attention to those deposits which are particularly ours, which have made us what we are, as a people, as a nation.

Yet no sooner have I said this than I want to stop and dig in my heels at the huge overestimation of the threat presently posed to our culture, or, worse still, our "identity"—a rather more elusive concept. In particular, the claim that "multiculturalism" is menacing our sense of who we are—American, English, or whatever—seems to me sinister and farcical in equal measure. Do the intellectuals who broadcast these grim vaticinations ever go to a football match? Can they not see how easily and strongly the modern nation exerts its grip upon the speech, manners, and loyalty of its citizens? Have they not the slightest inkling of, say, how indelibly American the most anti-American American activist, black or white, seems to any foreigner? The nationalist always has this strange split mind: the national identity seems to him incredibly important and yet at the same time woefully fragile, as though it were something both as precious and as easy to lose as the crease in his trousers is to a dandy.

Despite all predictions of increasing global homogeneity, as the years go by, the Americans become more American, the Canadians stay Canadian, the Australians remain Australian, and even the poor British retain not only their national characteristics, but many of these regional ones which the BBC was supposed to have ironed out a generation ago. Yorkshiremen, for example, retain the same stubbornness, the same awkward conceit of themselves as

they had in Tudor times; read Giraldus's comprehensive account of the characteristics of the Welsh in the twelfth century, and you could be in a Swansea pub in the 1990s.

Multiculturalism may be a threat to, say, the study of
literature in the academy, when second-rate works by
female black poets crowd out Melville and Hawthorne, but
as a threat to national consciousness, it seems to me to rank
pretty near zero.

The multicultural threat most often mentioned in the
United States—that of the Hispanic concentrations in
Florida and elsewhere in the South and Southwest—only
shows how feeble and illusory the threat really is, when
considered with any care. As Mark Falcoff has pointed out
in a recent essay (reprinted in the *Times Literary Supplement*
for May 17, 1996), the Hispanic culture cannot represent
any kind of long-term challenge to the dominance of English-speaking America, since it has no single mother
country to draw sustenance from (unlike the French in
Canada), it has no historic territorial base within the
United States, nor does speaking Spanish offer much of an
avenue to advancement for the next generation.

Cases where rival pasts have been unearthed and made
much of—as in Scotland, say—do not represent much of a
threat to the survival of the dominant, in our case the
English, past. On the contrary, particular revivals of this
type seem to be a part of a general revival of interest in all
our pasts. Never has the devotion to what survives of our
heritage been more ubiquitously imprinted on every tea
towel and backdropped into every television ad. Kitsch
no doubt, but if the tidal wave of kitsch the intellectual
Jeremiah claims we are drowning under includes the very
same nostalgia and sense of loss that the intellectual himself
feels (though vilely debased, of course), then he cannot

claim to be the sole *laudator temporis acti*, even if he alone may be able to translate the phrase.

Nor need this interest in the past be a passive, inert thing. On the contrary, for present-day novelists it is a driving obsession, a source of fantasy and comedy, a line of destiny to be traced like a lifeline in a hand, a wellspring of regret. There is hardly an English-speaking corner of the globe untouched by novelists grubbing for roots. In Canada, for example, Michael Ondaatje's *The English Patient* commutes between the last years of World War II and modern Toronto; Carol Shields in *The Stone Diaries* traces the hard destiny of a rural family from the nineteenth century to the present; Mordecai Richler's *Solomon Gursky Was Here* takes us from Sir John Franklin's search for the Northwest frontier through the bootleg years down to postwar plutocracy. Perhaps the more dazzling of all recent historical novels is E. Annie Proulx's *The Shipping News*, which "does" the Newfoundland coast so subtly that the novel does not even feel historical. In Australia, David Malouf and Thomas Keneally rehearse the same transition from a brutal, lawless pioneering to a soft, sleazy present, while Shena Mackay's *Dunedin* performs a comparable trick for the relationship between Britain and New Zealand. In Britain itself, there is a whole range of historical delving, from re-creations such as Peter Ackroyd's *Hawksmoor* and *Chatterton* to minuets between the past and the present such as John Fowles's *French Lieutenant's Woman* and A. S. Byatt's *Possession*. Not to mention Beryl Bainbridge's tableaux of the late nineteenth and early twentieth century, bringing back to life such resonant and tragic events as Scott's last journey and the sinking of the *Titanic*. And I have not begun to count the horde of precious and semi-precious stones streaming out of India and her diaspora:

the Naipaul brothers, Salman Rushdie, Vikram Seth, Rohinton Mistry, all in one way or another concerned with tracing the subcontinent's legacy to the world. A rough comparison with the fiction of the nineteenth and early twentieth century will show an engagement with the past which was far less intense and fruitful.

But while artists have always drawn strength and material from their national pasts, it should be clearly understood that it is not their task to succor or inflate national consciousness. The relationship is and ought to be the other way around: everything that goes into national feeling—language, landscape, history—flows into the artist, but as soon as the artist attempts to pump extra vitality back into national feeling, he is almost always betrayed into bad art. The great artist—Beethoven, Mann, Yeats—not only swiftly repents of any national-political celebration he may have been lured into but is unflinching in counting the cost to others:

> Did that play of mine send out
> Certain men the English shot.

Thus, of the four threats intertwined in the conservative lament, I worry about only one: the "dumbing down," which does represent a serious degradation of our educational standards, but which is ultimately remediable and which educational reforms, in Britain at least, have some hope of reversing over the course of a generation, for the simple reason that the majority of parents will not tolerate another lost generation.

Of the other three threats, I think little. Vulgarization is an incapable consequence of democracy; it has its blowsy charms; and in certain forms, it can act as a bulwark of our political traditions. Nor do I think the past is dying away from our minds; on the contrary, there is a widespread longing that it should be more vividly present to us. Still less do I think that any of our national identities is under threat. Multiculturalism is at worst a congeries of small sillinesses and at best a form of courtesy to insecure immigrants. But here is a further kind of loss which we in Britain suffered a long time ago and which is not much mentioned. Of all the threats to culture in Britain, the only one that seems to have any real substance is the loss of our common European heritage.

From the 1880s on, perhaps much earlier if we are to believe Matthew Arnold, British culture cut itself off and developed into something defensive, provincial, parochial even, tame. Two world wars helped to reinforce our insularity and cultural autarky. Decade by decade, we lost the old ease of intellectual commerce across the whole continent of Europe, that sense of belonging to a common conversation.

This is certainly *not* to say that the European Union, either now or in the future, is going to be a leading element in rekindling that conversation. In its cultural efforts, the European Union is a sort of well-meaning Euro-Disney, attempting to homogenize what is neither homogenous nor homogeneous, and generalizing what is of its essence particular. Nonetheless, the European Union does provide an essential underpinning. Little by little, the Single European Market and the habits of daily negotiation within the EU, however fractious and time consuming, begin to make the old insularity look absurd.

That is not how the conservative press in Britain sees it, but then, to the rest of Europe and to a large part of the British public, the conservative press and the Euro-phobes seem absurd—not wrong necessarily on important practical issues, such as monetary union—but absurd, nonetheless. And their attempts to compare the EU with Napoleon's empire or Hitler's are as deranged as comparing the Athenaeum club with Auschwitz.

Yet perhaps the nationalists in the Conservative Party are not as stupid as they seem. Perhaps there is some ulterior wisdom in their prickly refusal of any further entanglement with the Continent. If we keep ourselves to ourselves, then perhaps we can retain our illusions about ourselves in general, and about our high culture in particular.

We can go on believing that our stale and timid figurative painters are great masters in the European tradition, that Elgar is a great composer, that A. S. Byatt is as good as Gabriel García Márquez—but the catalogue is too depressing to rehearse. I greatly enjoy the conservative attack on the cheap, phony, and derivative stuff served up by certain fashionable artists and writers, the purveyors of piss and excrement, the glorifiers of mutilation and corpse-kissing, these stale spinoffs of Duchamp and Artaud, but I cannot help noticing an uneasy silence when, say, one turns to that excellent periodical *Modern Painters* to see what the cultural conservative would bring forward in their stead. I recall, for example, the exhibition "Paradise Lost" at the Barbican Gallery, a retrospective of the British neo-Romantic art of the 1940s. Charming and infinitely evocative as it was, again and again one could not shut one's eyes to the sheer technical incompetence, the feebleness of the draftsmanship, the timidity of conception, the easy sentimentality. The traditional culture that we are so eager to defend has run thin in places—and, to put it no higher, we may suspect that its walling-off within the compound of the nation hasn't helped.

There is quite a lot to be said against the "multiculturalist novel," for example, most of which we are too
polite to say: that it achieves some of its comic and piquant
effects through cheap juxtapositions (of white speech and
manners alongside the half-mangled, half-parodied im-
migrant versions), that many of its themes—rootlessness,
relativism, alienation—are rather glibly exploited, that it
lacks human depth. One may say all this, yet one then has
to turn to the *echt*-British article and look hard, very hard,
to find the same exuberance and energy, the same sense of
engaging, however cack-handedly, with the times that you
find in Salman Rushdie and Timothy Mo.

Nor does this kind of critique apply to art alone, although it is in the arts that its effect is most conspicuous,
because artists can up sticks when they fear their native
culture is stifling them—by its dullness, its pride in its
limitations, its suspicions. Though never a keen admirer of
D. H. Lawrence, I remember how struck I was on first
reading his piece *Dull London*: "the first half-hour in London after some years abroad, is really a plunge of misery.
The strange, the grey and the uncanny, almost deathly sense
of *dullness* is overwhelming." Of course, England was the
easiest country in the world and the English people the
nicest:

> But this very easiness and this very niceness become at last
> a nightmare. It is as if the whole air were impregnated
> with chloroform or some other pervasive anesthetic, that
> makes everything easy and nice, and takes the edge off
> everything, whether nice or nasty. As you inhale the drug
> of easiness and niceness, your vitality begins to sink. Per-
> haps not your physical vitality, but something else: the
> vivid flame of your individual life.

Lawrence was ill, dying in fact, and even when he had been well, he was always a monumental complainer. Yet his impatience still hits a nerve, and you begin to remember why English writers and artists used to live abroad.

Politicians and jurists are by their trade confined to their own country. Yet unless refreshed by dialogue with other traditions, they too lose critical edge. I fervently believe in and have great affection for our British methods of proceeding by precedent, by attending to each case as it comes, yet there are historical moments when we need to raise our hearts from the casebook and sniff the outside air; the impact of European institutions upon our law and Parliament is only one example, though a striking one, of our failure to engage with the realities of the modern world. We joined the Common Market over twenty years ago, yet the House of Commons has only this summer begun to demand that an English text of every proposal be laid before them and the minister responsible come to be questioned before going to Brussels to decide the matter. We signed the European Convention of Human Rights over forty years ago; most English and Scottish judges now treat it as an informal part of our law, yet Parliament still refuses to enact it into law, which means that cases brought under the Convention still have to go, at huge expense, to Strasburg, instead of being decided in the first instance by British judges. The pretense of self-sufficiency is a costly one and, because it is only a pretense, ultimately enervating, leading to inevitable frustration and resentment.

This is not a critique of high British culture alone. Conservative critics in France, such as Marc Fumaroli and George Liébert, make much the same critique of their situation. The same lament can be heard in Germany, too, and in China and a half-dozen other countries. Nor is it an unqualified or wholehearted critique; it is one which would take a good deal more arguing.

It is relevant here for one reason only: that it provokes, in me at any rate, an uncomfortable suspicion that conservatives on both sides of the Atlantic like to lament the destruction of the past when what they are secretly, perhaps unconsciously, lamenting is the exhaustion of the present. It is easier these days to identify an enemy than a hero, but then perhaps it always was.

Yet, I am reluctant to sign off with an ironic whimper, a limply raised eyebrow. Some plain things are worth saying plainly: that more or less democratic governments are today well entrenched from the Atlantic to the Urals; that the discontent with the European Union is, in comparison with this great circumstance (unique in our century or any other), a fairly secondary matter; that the threat of neonationalism, though ugly, is also minor, being mostly a reaction to the piping times of peace, and not confined to nations crammed together in unwelcome supranational associations (it's happening in Japan and a dozen other countries too); that, when we turn to the arts, we find a situation not unprecedented, namely that some of them appear stalled up a cul-de-sac, while others—the novel, architecture, perhaps poetry—are producing work which often stirs and occasionally captivates. It is possible, if you try hard enough, to find people still spouting the old rubbish—for example, that the Cold War was not worth winning, that the family is dying or ought to be, that art is nothing if it is not revolutionary—but where I come from, people who say these things are greeted with yawns.

One may reproach the European present with many things—a lack of ambition, a devitalized sort of wariness.

But we might also describe these qualities as the defects of our virtues: we may seem disenchanted because we have most of us ceased to be enchanted by cruel and fatuous ideologies.

To say this is not to express some kind of reach-me-down optimism (somewhere under the dead leaves new growth is stirring). On the contrary, the greatest cause for optimism in Europe is that there is so little optimism about, for optimism implies some degree of self-satisfaction. And perhaps the regrowth of interest in all our pasts comes not so much from a sentimental urge to recapture something we have lost as from a feeling that we ought to retrace our path in order to see where we went wrong. Perhaps we should have followed Gladstone, not Marx; William James rather than Freud; Arnold Bennett, not Virginia Woolf; Lutyens, not Le Corbusier. In our voyage of rediscovery, we shall need more accurate instruments of navigation and a log that is better kept. But for most of us, the past still has work to do.

January 1997

Possessing the Golden Key

John Herington

Prelude: Decline & Fall

STUDENTS of the ancient classics have this in common
with fishermen: they are often to be overheard lamenting the much bigger one that got away—the loss, long ago,
of entire literary genres, or of once-famous masterpieces
like Aeschylus's tragic trilogy on Achilles and Patroklos, or
Ennius's thunderous epic on the history of Rome. More
than the students of most other subjects, they are forced
to be constantly aware of the appalling fragility of culture.
There are reminders at every turn, even if one is only faced
with a mutilated sentence in a poem or with a gap in a
temple frieze, of how much was lost and the way it was
lost, whether through indifference or ignorance or deliberate malice. Hence it seems reasonable, before speculating
on the future of the classical component in the European
past, to consider whether any hints can be found in a great
classical student's vision of the cultural collapse of the classical world. Here is a passage from Wilamowitz, the con-
summator of the grand tradition of German classical scholarship, on the Roman Empire at the apparent height of
its material prosperity and power in the second century of
our era:

How does it help that this period brims over with General
Education, from which no mountain glen in Lycia, no
African country town can be secure—that the Imperial
post runs from Lisbon to Palmyra—that roads are paved
and aqueducts erected, along with tasteful chapels and
country houses, and statues in the style of Thutmose the
Third or Nebuchadnezzar or Peisistratos, and Euriposes
and Kanoposes and Mausoleums? It is the spirit alone that
lives and creates life; but the spirit is not mocked, and far
more evil and more barbaric than the periods in which it
has not yet awakened are those in which it has vanished
away, and has to be shammed.

And what happens in a period when the spirit has to be
shammed? As Wilamowitz goes on to indicate, there is no
immediate, obvious catastrophe; that comes later. There is
simply a general erosion. Among other arts, the literature
of the past is no longer sought out for its own life-giving
properties, but retreats from life into the schools, and by
them is naturally cut down to manageable and teachable
proportions. A few, a very few, texts are selected for classroom use, and these are in a manner embalmed by elaborate paraphrases and interpretations, to make them intelligible to the now uninterested students. About this same
period, as Wilamowitz supposed, some deservedly nameless
pedagogue (or could it possibly have been a committee
convoked by some antique equivalent of a dean?) arrived at
decisions about the Greek syllabus whose effects are with us
to the present day: students should be required to read only
seven dramas by Aeschylus, for instance, out of more than
eighty; and likewise only seven out of the more than a
hundred and twenty composed by Sophocles. Bearing in
mind the fate of classical literature in the final centuries of

the Empire, one may be tempted to formulate a universal rule: the anthologists arrive within the walls a century or so before the barbarians; people who have once lost the habit of going out and reading for themselves will gradually lose the capacity to love what they read or even to understand it. At least the rule may be worth testing against the conditions of our own time. It may be added that the teachers of those people, correspondingly, may before long become lost in trivialities themselves, like those scholars at the very end of classical antiquity who were to be found (as the phrase goes) "arguing over the vocative of *ego* amid the crash of empires."

Renaissances

Yet there is something else of which a classics student is inevitably aware, simply in the pursuit of his or her trade, and that is the latent vitality and attractive power of the Greco-Roman culture. There have been many times since its collapse during which its arts, visual and written, even in partial ruin, have awoken a passionate urge not merely to enjoy or imitate them but to assimilate them, and to raise a new culture on their foundations. Perhaps Goethe's breathless response to a mere black and white drawing of an original Greek sculpture may stand as typical of innumerable responses, across the ages, to classical work: "It is a fathomless depth of wisdom and strength; one becomes at once 2000 years younger and better; there's no more to say; come and see!" At many points in history, as we all know, there have been flare-ups of this sort in societies as well as individuals: at the court of Charlemagne, for instance, and in twelfth-century France and England, and above all the great European conflagration that broke out in fourteenth-century Italy and smoldered, here and there, at least into the early part of the present century. During that greatest of renaissances, the classical component in European civilization was so strong and pervasive—even when its achievements were transcended, even when they were rebelled against—that no definition of European identity could fail to take it into account. Classical literature and art, and the postclassical literature and art of Europe, formed a continuum, the one not truly intelligible without the other.

The war of 1914–18, above all, put an end to that. If there now exists such a thing as a European identity—a European present to set against the European past that is the subject of this book—I doubt if anybody would claim that classical influence is a significant element in it. As will shortly be seen, some people are continuing to study the classical world, with great intensity, in North America as well as in Europe. Whether their activity is likely to facilitate yet another renaissance, in any way comparable to those we have seen before, is the ultimate question before this essay.

Crystal Gazing in 1997

Back in the 1960s, when computers were just beginning to make an impact on society at large, some conservative-minded wit put about the rumor that a new device of titanic power had just been developed. It was the key to everything you could possibly need to know, and yet it could be carried in the hand and needed no cords or batteries; it had no name as yet, but provisionally it was being called Built-in Orderly Organized Knowledge, or BOOK for short. The assumption behind this joke had of course prevailed in Western civilization since the days of the Hellenistic Greeks; no doubt the most famous example of it is in the last canto of the *Divine Comedy*, where the universe in all its knowable aspects is envisioned as a codex whose scattered leaves are bound together in God.

Three decades later, that assumption is no longer secure. Anyone who sets out to predict any aspect of future society must begin by acknowledging that we are now in the midst of a cultural transition compared to which the transitions from oral to written literature, and from manuscript to print, may prove to have been quite minor affairs. When the elementary schools are being wired for the Internet, who knows what is about to happen, for good or ill, to the entire educational and social structure? Is the book likely to preserve its primacy, or even, in the long run, its existence as an instrument of education or entertainment? Will the *word* (whether spoken or printed or just looming greenly on a computer screen) be able to make headway against the roaring torrent of visual images? Even in daily life the visual image seems to be taking over from the alphabet: if you want to dine, to escape a fire, or to find a lavatory, reading will not always help: you must learn to decipher pictograms, which in these emergencies will be crossed eating-irons, zigzag lines, and skirted or trousered silhouettes respectively.

At this stage, then, there can be no certainty about the future of the European past, or of the classical component in it. We may be heading toward the ultimate intellectual and aesthetic renaissance, toward a universal volume where all that human beings have achieved is present at the touch of a key—and the European past is really not a negligible part of what has been achieved. Or we may be heading toward nothing of the kind, but rather toward an infinitude of Platonic caves where lonely watchers sit under constraint, poring over a procession of shadows. My present assignment would have been very much easier to carry out in 1597, or even in 1897, than it is at this moment. Nonetheless, I shall here attempt a short-term forecast, working forward as best I can from my observation of the present state of affairs.

The Future of the Classical Past, I: Image & Translation

When once seen, the visual arts of the classical world, and the very landscapes and seascapes in which they are set, hardly require a propagandist. Most people, I think, at least those whose perceptions have not been skewed by educational ideologues, can fully understand the response of Goethe to his drawing of a Greek sculpture. All that is needed is what in Goethe's time was limited to a tiny elite, namely accessibility. Even now reproductions of unprecedented quality are widely available in that conventional medium, the book, to anyone who cares to consult a public library. Still greater wonders are being performed for ancient art and topography by electronic means; one need only refer to the Yale University Press's Perseus Project, with its vast computerized repertoire of images relating to ancient Greece. In this age of images, everything suggests that we are to expect more, much more, of the same kind of production. Everyman may before long take his stand with Zeus on the top of a virtual Mount Olympus, or build his own virtual Parthenon, reunited at last, virtually, with its Elgin Marbles.

The classical writers, too, have in recent years become more accessible in translation than at any time in history, particularly in the English-speaking world. The outpouring of English translations since the Second World War far surpasses in bulk that earlier great outpouring at the height of the English Renaissance, in the reigns of Elizabeth and James. It must at once be admitted, however, that the stylistic quality of the modern translations is extremely variable. The Elizabethans and Jacobeans knew instinctively how to make poetry sing in English, and prose, too, come to that (one thinks not only of Sandys' Ovid, for instance, but also of Holland's Plutarch). They could therefore match, to some extent, the verbal harmonies that have always made Homer or Cicero so incomparably attractive to anyone lucky enough to read them in their own languages. It is forgotten, by many contemporary translators and by almost all their reviewers, that the ancient civilizations put as much sustained collective effort into the shaping of sentences and ver⸻ ⸺⸺ ⸻⸺ the shaping of stone and clay, and ⸻⸺⸺ ⸻⸺ ⸺m as much in the one medium ⸻⸺ ⸺⸺ ⸻ presents the world with a trans⸻ ⸻⸺ ⸻ into cacophonous jargon disp⸻ ⸻⸺ gth posing as verses may possib⸻ ⸻ of the poet's storyline, but le⸻ ⸻he is presenting that poet, or su⸻ ⸻as excited the ages.

Although translators in gene⸻ ould probably be held to a higher critical standard than they are, I find myself still very hopeful for the future of classical literature in translation. Two recent developments, in particular, and their wider effects, will be worth watching. The ongoing Oxford University Press series, The Greek Tragedy in New Translations, was founded by the late William Arrowsmith on the undeniable premise that not every classical scholar is gifted as a creative writer, and that few creative writers now have leisure for the prolonged savoring of the classics in the original. There are of course exceptions (the most out-standing one being no doubt Arrowsmith himself), and a few volumes in the new series are in fact by a single in-dividual; most, however, are the combined work of a pro-fessional Hellenist and a professional poet. The results of these collaborations naturally vary from play to play, but the volumes that have appeared have this in common, that they are in a credible, speakable, rhythmic English able to capture the attention and feelings of a contemporary au-dience. There seems to be a very strong case for extending this principle of collaboration from the translation of the tragedies to that of other classical literature in verse and prose. It is the abounding *life* of the ancient writings that strikes even a beginning reader in the original lan-guages, and those who know how to put life into our own language should surely be invited to share in translating them.

An equally promising development is the practice of publishing classical translations not only in books but also in audio tapes. Of course many works of literature from all ages and civilizations are now available on tape, but it may not yet be generally realized that to tape a classical poem or speech is a great deal more than merely to make it available to people too indolent to read, or people driving across the continent: it is in itself a necessary act of re-creative scholarship, since it means restoring the classical work to the very environment for which it was designed in the first place, namely the airwaves. One easily forgets that in Ro-man as well as in Greek culture most of what we call lit-erature, though preserved by books, was realized in oral delivery. Oscar Wilde rightly explained one aspect of the excellence of Greek literature (being in this matter well ahead of the educational practice of his time) in these words: "The test was always the spoken word in its musical and metrical relations. The voice was the medium, and the ear the critic." Hence to me, at least, the tapes published by Penguin Audiobooks of Robert Fagles's *Iliad* translation recited by the actor Derek Jacobi was one of the great classical breakthroughs of recent years, because it restored to Homer's poetry its full dramatic force, its interplay of human and divine voices, for the first time (so far as my knowledge goes) since the performances of the ancient Greek rhapsodes. The tapes of Fagles's *Odyssey*,[1] recited by Ian McKellen, have also been recently released; but indeed every classical poem, speech, and history, as well as many works of philosophy such as the shorter dialogues of Plato, would respond wonderfully to a recording by a trained professional actor (we should no doubt want to draw the line at such technical works as Aristotle's *Categories* or Frontinus's *On the Aqueducts of Rome*).

Given speakable translations and interested actors, there is no reason why the entire corpus of classical literature should not be available in glorious sound, whether in audio recordings or on the Internet or both, within a few years. It may be added that a great many Greek classical texts—accompanied by the not-so-speakable translations found in the Loeb Classical Library—are currently available in the Perseus Project already mentioned, alongside the many images of the art, architecture, and sites. We seem, in fact, to be well within reach of a future in which all of classical

---

1 *The Odyssey*, by Homer. Translated by Robert Fagles. Recorded on twelve audio cassettes by Ian McKellen (Penguin Audiobooks).

culture will be present to anybody who wants it, freely, at the touch of a key.

Interlude: "But the Spirit Is Not Mocked"?

At this very point, perhaps, the thoughtful reader may uneasily recall Wilamowitz's vision of the second century A.D., quoted in the prelude to this essay. There, too, was a world united from one end to the other by the same material culture and the same education, a world in which (so far as the technology of the time allowed) all the achievements of past civilization were reproduced and placed at everyone's disposal—the statues in the Egyptian taste, or the Babylonian, or the archaic Greek, adorning comfortable villas, the ornamental canals and monuments modeled on this or that famous tourist site in Greece or the Near East. How little real commitment to the masterpieces of the past survived behind the imperial facade was to become clear before very long, as the general erosion of ancient literature accelerated. It may seem that the real, the lasting culture is that which one has to go out and get for oneself, perhaps through great labor; not that which has to be laid on, piped in from outside like the water through the giant aqueducts.

The Future of the Classical Past, II: The Golden Key

In the sixty-sixth chapter of his *Decline and Fall*, as he approached the reign of the last Emperor of the East and the fall of Constantinople in 1453, Edward Gibbon at long last rendered his judgment on the Greek language. He did so in

a majestic sentence whose incantatory, almost psalmlike quality is best brought out if it is transcribed as verse:

> In their lowest servitude and depression,
> the subjects of the Byzantine throne
>   were still possessed
> of a golden key that could unlock the treasures of antiquity;
> of a musical and prolific language,
>   that gives
> a soul to the objects of sense
> and a body to the abstractions of philosophy.

Everyone who has managed to read even a little ancient
Greek philosophy or poetry in the original will, I think, feel
the complete justice of this description. But it also serves as
a most powerful reminder that in the last resort it is language that lies nearest to the heart, whatever society, whatever literature is under study. The future integrity of classical studies, if not their survival, depends ultimately on
the future of Greek and Latin learning. Only if such learning continues can we look forward to genuine, firsthand
research, or count on the honesty of future translations.
Much the same, of course, will apply to the study of any
of the other great national literatures that have arisen on
the European continent; the future of the European past
generally seems to be bound up with the future of language
studies.

At a first glance, the promise for Greek and Latin language studies in the computer age seems bright indeed.
CD-ROMs that make it possible to summon up every single
occurrence of a given word, or collocation of words, in all
extant classical Latin and Greek literature have already been
available to students for several years, and we confidently

expect the system to be vastly improved in the near future, with additions and corrections and with the extension of the chronological coverage into the medieval period and perhaps beyond. This resource alone means that the beginner who has just learned the Greek alphabet can instantly command more Greek (in a certain sense) than earlier scholars could command after a lifetime's engagement with the texts. Similarly, the ongoing project of electronically storing the secondary literature on the classics will mean that what was once perhaps the crowning skill of the veteran scholar—the ability to say where a treatment of a given subject may be found—is now fully in the beginner's hands. There is already a Latin bulletin board on the Internet (see *The New York Times*, October 28, 1996), and nothing that I can see prevents the establishment of an ancient Greek board, or of any other aids to self-improvement in the ancient languages, such as beginning or advanced courses in them.

Yet it has historically been true, and may well remain so, that most people require an academic infrastructure to support them in the long and laborious process of mastering the ins and outs of a great literary language. Paradoxically, the academic infrastructure for the study of Latin and Greek is at present far more extensive in America than it is in any European country. Since the Second World War, on both sides of the Atlantic, the study has been retreating from the high schools into the colleges and universities. Greek is taught only to a few high-school-age pupils, too often in devoted groups working unofficially on their own time. Latin, at any rate in the United States, is still widely taught at the high-school level but, by my observation, under serious difficulties; I have known gifted and spirited teachers almost reduced to despair by the pressure from parents and administrators to simplify the language to the extent that the whole exercise becomes meaningless.

As one might expect, conditions at the college and university level vary widely from country to country. In several European countries, the study of Latin and Greek seems practically confined to the graduate school and the research institute, touching the average educated person no more closely than, say, cuneiform studies or Old Church Slavic. In the United States, on the other hand, most colleges and universities at present offer undergraduate majors in one or both of the classical languages. For various inescapable causes, this language instruction is no doubt less concentrated and strenuous than it was a couple of generations back, but a talented undergraduate can still work wonders with it. The United States can also boast far more numerous, and on the whole better attended, graduate departments of classics than can Europe. And it is perhaps here above all, in the graduate schools and in the professional teachers of classical learning who emerge from them, that we may best divine the future of the classical past. They are the key-bearers.

An innocent observer of the professional scene will probably be struck, first of all, by the enormous bulk of books and articles about the classics that professors, and even their graduate students, are now pouring from the presses. Never at any previous epoch in the long history of classical studies—not in Hellenistic Alexandria, for instance, not in Wilhelmine Germany—has there ever been anything remotely approaching such an output. Yet what might on a superficial view be taken for proof of an unequaled prosperity may actually prove a near-fatal weakness. The unfortunate fact is that almost every working scholar I know, whether beginner or veteran, agrees that most of this voluminous writing is useless and indeed worse than useless—that the enforced production of it discourages the necessary prolonged apprenticeship in the Greek and Latin languages, narrows the individual, and may yet stifle the profession. The time has probably come to examine very closely the two great requirements that now confront all prospective teachers of the classics at the university or college level: the writing of a dissertation before the conferring of a degree, and the early publication of a considerable quantity of other work either contemporaneously with the dissertation or shortly thereafter.

In nineteenth-century Germany, the classical dissertation was on the whole an effective device for ensuring that a student, after many years of instruction at the school and university levels, was master of his trade and able to concentrate his learning on the solution of some hitherto unexplored problem in the classical field. Transplanted lock, stock, and barrel into the United States during the latter part of the century, the dissertation requirement at first worked fairly well, but increasingly, as time has gone by, it has begun to suffer from two difficulties: objectively soluble problems of any significance have become harder and harder to find (except in certain specialties such as epigraphy, papyrology, or linguistics); and the graduate student has been arriving at the dissertation with less and less preliminary training in Greek or Latin or the many subdisciplines that a classical scholar needs. Happily, there will always be one or two students who can astound their tutors by overcoming even such odds as these, and one still occasionally runs into a dissertation that truly contributes to knowledge and that has truly broadened its author's education. Yet on the whole the graduate student in classics is nowadays condemned to spend his or her last two or more years in graduate school—those priceless years which should allow leisure, for the only time in one's life, to assimilate the literature one has studied and to deepen one's acquaintance with other literature as well—in raking through a pile of practically unreadable secondary writing concerning the chosen topic of the dissertation and hectically trying to extract therefrom some fact, or some idea, that no one has hit on.

It seems that alternatives to this system ought to be under serious scrutiny by everyone who is concerned with the future of the classical past (or, I need hardly say by this time in the argument, with the future of academic studies in any area of language or literature). The best suggestion that I have heard of was put forward by William Arrowsmith years ago, at the University of Texas in Austin. It was simply that classicists should follow the example of some architecture schools, and allow those students who so wished to submit not a dissertation but a portfolio illustrating their work in its various aspects. Such a portfolio, he suggested, might contain proof of the student's understanding of the ancient languages, and of his own, in the form of original compositions in Latin and Greek, and well meditated, stylistically acceptable English translations from passages in the classics; one or more brief investigative articles on restricted problems not yet widely written on by the specialists; and one or more essays on history, or literary or artistic criticism. The idea, I think, might be worth experimenting with.

If only the problems ceased with the acceptance of the dissertation, as for a long time they did, the present system might be just tolerable. At that point, if no earlier, our new member of the profession would be free to read more widely and deeply, and to consider at leisure where to go next in his or her research and teaching. In the last twenty-five years, all that has changed. Not only the major research universities but all institutions, including those devoted primarily to undergraduate teaching, have begun to expect even applicants for beginning positions or one-year temporary positions to have one or more published articles to their credit; while the aspirant to a tenured position is required (apart from many other qualifications) to be able to boast of one or even two published books, plus a number of articles. The results are obvious. There is the enormous outpouring of unnecessary publication, scarcely to be kept track of even with electronic help, that has already been mentioned—a mass of material towering ever higher between the observer and the prime objects of his or her observation, the original texts or the original stones. In the same process, the good work that is done (and of course there is much good work) is obscured and choked out by the mediocre. As if all that were not damage enough, the narrowing effect of the dissertation requirement is now prolonged seven or even ten years further into our professor's teaching career. After he or she has achieved tenure, one must hope for the best. It is hard not to recall the Full Professor in Howard Nemerov's poem:

> Publish or perish! What a frightful chance!
> It troubled him through all his early days.
> But now he has the system beat both ways;
> He publishes and perishes at once.

But even if our professor escapes that cruel fate, his or her energies will from then on be increasingly distracted from the real job by the barren duty of reviewing the mounting pile of secondary literature turned out by aspirants to the profession. Such, I think, are the main threats posed to Greek and Latin studies under the present system of appointment and promotion.

Even so, as far as one can reasonably foresee in 1997, factual knowledge about the classical past and the classical languages is likely to remain available in future to anybody who happens to want it. We are probably not about to lose any more masterpieces, as they did in the dying centuries of the Roman Empire. It is another question whether the academic infrastructure as it now stands can adequately support the masterpieces we have, allowing them to exert their full power on society, to mold its style and spark its imagination in yet another of that long series of renaissances. Outside the academy there are signs that such a renaissance is at least within the bounds of possibility; a reader of Seamus Heaney's *The Cure at Troy* or Derek Walcott's *Omeros* may well feel hopeful even now.

February 1997

The Real Stuff of History

Keith Windschuttle

I F an Oxford don had set out in the 1960s on the formidable task of writing a history of the world in the last millennium, almost certainly his main theme would have been the rise to dominance of the West, especially in the areas of science, politics, and economic and military power. This would have been true no matter which side he supported in the great ideological divide of the Cold War. Both the political Left and the Right had little doubt the West was the vanguard of history. The major Asian civilizations might have held vastly greater populations but for at least five hundred out of the past thousand years they had been on the receiving end of the great historical movements of the era rather than out in front, setting the pace.

In the Sixties, the history of Asia would have been written as something of a tragedy, a story of opportunities lost, of the closing of minds, of political weakness and disintegration. China, in particular, would have been treated as a sorry case, a country that began the millennium technologically advanced, wealthy, politically and militarily powerful, keenly interested in navigation and exploration, but which ended the era as one of the most backward countries in the world on almost every one of these scores, its population decimated by famine and ruled by an inept tyranny. In contrast, the small fiefdoms that constituted

Christendom in the eleventh century had risen to become masters of the world, with their populations wealthy beyond belief, well-educated, and spread around the globe, throughout Western Europe, the Americas, and Oceania.

How things have changed within thirty years! I am not, mind you, referring to the reality of the comparative distribution of wealth, intelligence, and power in the world, but to the way our Oxford don would address his subject matter in the 1990s. Professor Felipe Fernández-Armesto, a member of the modern history faculty of that university, has provided in his recent book *Millennium: A History of the Last Thousand Years*[1] just such a dramatic reappraisal. He sees the old version of the story reflecting not the truth about global influence but merely the inflated egocentrism of Western commentators. The imagined dominance of the West was "later, feebler and briefer than is commonly supposed," he claims, and was "neither foreordained nor enduring." Rather than China being the great loser of the period, the author sees the most stable feature of the past millennium as "an almost continuous history of Chinese preponderance." Europe has been but "a small promontory of Asia." The latter is where the most important and lasting business of humanity has been taking place all this time. Moreover, at the end of this millennium, he says, the brief initiative enjoyed by the West is now returning to the shores of the Pacific. So, he begins and ends his book with the achievements of the civilizations of Asia, especially Japan and China.

Throughout the text, he rebukes Western ethnocentrism at almost every opportunity. Not for him the assessment by

---

1 *Millennium: A History of the Last Thousand Years*, by Felipe Fernández-Armesto (Touchstone Books).

Adam Smith that the two most important historical events of the last thousand years were the decision of the Portuguese to round the Cape of Good Hope and open a trade route to India, and the funding by Spain's Ferdinand and Isabella of the voyage of Christopher Columbus to America. No, both events were overshadowed even in their own day by the expansion of the Ottoman Empire into the Mediterranean, by far the most world shattering imperial expansion of the fifteenth century, he maintains. Moreover, the rise of capitalism in Western Europe was neither unique nor as momentous as economic historians and theorists like to imagine. Up to the early nineteenth century, for instance, the merchants of Canton were vastly richer than those of Europe. Wu Ping-Chien could have bought and sold banking empires like that of the Rothschilds several times over, he claims. It was only through military victory in the Opium War of 1839–42 that the European "barbarians" and "parasites" (his terminology) managed to claw back the difference. Eventually, he notes with satisfaction, the gains the British made on Chinese territory turned out to be but transitory toeholds.

This kind of approach dominates Fernández-Armesto's methodology of selection and judgment about what is important. The most prominent individuals who bestride his historic stage turn out to be those people most of us had regarded as the losers and has-beens. For instance, he has several pages about Montezuma but no mention of Ferdinand and Isabella. He devotes more space to Juan and Eva Perón than to Abraham Lincoln and Franklin Roosevelt combined. He has more pages on Mao Tse-tung and Joseph Stalin than any other political figures in the book, despite the fact that neither built a Communist regime that survived more than one generation beyond his own death.

St. Elizabeth of Hungary gets a mention but Elizabeth I of England gets none. As for Western intellectuals, neither Francis Bacon, John Locke, David Hume, nor Immanuel Kant are discussed at all. Neither Mozart nor Michelangelo make the team. The index does not list the category "philosophy" but does contain thirteen pages of references to shamans and shamanism. Most of the individuals Fernández-Armesto writes about are selected for their literary interest, because of what they reveal about the cultures he is describing or because they enliven the story with idiosyncrasies and paradoxical behaviors. Only a minority are there because they have been powerful or influential enough to affect the course of history, that is, to *change* history.

Though he eschews the kind of simplicities familiarly associated with theoretical or sociological explanations of history (he easily demolishes, for example, the thesis that the Protestant work ethic created capitalism), the author is operating with his own version of the great impersonal forces that change the fortunes of nations. His thesis is that the fate of civilizations has been defined by the seas and that the current of world history has shifted over the last thousand years from the China Sea to the Mediterranean, then to the Atlantic and now back again to the Pacific Rim. Crucial to his story are the opportunities provided by things like the direction of the prevailing winds, the navigability of the rivers, the quality of the climate, and the nature of the topography. Compared to these great forces of destiny, the impact of the Alexanders, the Caesars, and the Napoleons of the world, and the political influence of systems such as democracy, autocracy, and bureaucracy, have been puny.

As the year 2000 approaches, *Millennium*, a generously illustrated book of 816 pages published simultaneously in several translated editions, is the first of what is likely to be a number of its kind. It should have been a matter of some satisfaction that a well-accredited scholar like Fernández-Armesto had got in so early to set the standard for the genre. Instead, this book and its inevitable imitators tell us far less about the real fate of humanity in the last thousand years and far more about what has gone wrong with the writing of history in recent decades. *Millennium* was published in 1995 but written between 1991 and 1993. This timing seems to be part of its author's problem. He began writing at the end of the economic boom of the 1980s which saw both Japan and newly capitalist China set record-breaking economic growth rates that appeared to be recasting the order of the world's wealth and power. What should have been apparent to any historian taking the long view, of course, was that such bubbles usually burst. By the time Fernández-Armesto had finished writing, economic recession in Japan and runaway inflation in China had removed the aura of apparent economic invincibility from both countries and had reduced their prospects from the celestial to a more earthly level. In this sense, the symbol the author chooses in his prologue to show how the world has changed so dramatically—a London restaurant which used to serve French food but now offers Japanese—is only too appropriate. Today, in all the major Western cities, fashions in ethnic food change as rapidly as fashions in clothing. The restaurateur who switches his menus and decor from one cuisine to another is making the most trivial comment possible about the shifting stakes of world power.

There is, however, a malaise at work here far more crippling than the common mistake of assuming the short-term detours of one's own time have set the long-term course of the future. Fernández-Armesto's book is an agglomeration of several of the most debilitating tendencies that have emerged in the writing of history since the Second World War. Some of these afflictions have been political, especially the tendency to diminish our European past and to elevate that of just about every other part of the globe, no matter what the record. Others have been methodological, the adoption of practices in historical research and writing that have complemented these political judgments and without which, indeed, the political points could not have been made. Ironically enough, the worst methodological offenders have been the practitioners of the most nationally chauvinistic of all the post-1945 European schools of history, that of France. The writer upon whom Fernández-Armesto has most modeled his work is the French historian Fernand Braudel, the editor from 1956 until his death in 1985 of the journal *Annales d'histoire économique et sociale*. Braudel has written great tomes about periods almost as expansive as the millennium itself, including the huge three-volume *Civilisation and Capitalism 15th–18th Century* and the two-volume *The Identity of France*, which stretches from Roman Gaul to the Second World War.

Like the other practitioners of the *Annales* school, Braudel describes himself as a "structuralist historian," although his work is sometimes also called "total history." The term "structuralism" derives from anthropology and emphasizes not the cut and thrust of historical action but the purported framework, or underlying constants, that govern what action takes place. While other French historians of similar persuasion, such as Michel Foucault, describe the underlying framework as ideological, Braudel claims it is geographical. The first half of the book that made his name,

The Mediterranean and the Mediterranean World in the Age of Philip II (1949), is devoted to the role of the environment in the late sixteenth century, with chapters on objects such as peninsulas, mountains, plateaux, plains, seas, coasts, and climate. Only in his second half does the author stoop to focus upon the affairs of man, but even here he is mainly interested in trends in demography, trade balances, transportation, and social classes. Though Philip II of Spain is acknowledged in the book's title, this is merely to date the period under discussion. Braudel regards monarchs as interesting only in that they represent the category "monarchy." Philip himself left no mark of substance on his era. "Peasants and crops," the author assures us, "food supplies and the size of the population, silently determined the destiny of the age." With Braudel as editor, the *Annales* often expressed its scorn for the staples of the prewar discipline: political history, narrative, and episodic history. Under his influence, typical articles published in the journal would be entitled "The History of Rain and Fine Weather," and "Amenorrhoea in Time of Famine: Seventeenth to Twentieth Century." Part of the package that comes with this view of how to write history is the notion that particular historic events are of little consequence since they cannot influence, but merely express, the great underlying forces that cause them. "Resounding events often take place in an instant," Braudel writes in *The Mediterranean*, "and are but manifestations of that larger destiny by which alone they can be explained." Similarly, the role of the individual in history is hardly worthy of notice:

When I think of the individual, I am always inclined to see him imprisoned within a destiny in which he himself has little hand, fixed in a landscape in which the infinite perspectives of the long term, *la longue durée*, stretch into the distance both behind him and before. In historical analysis, as I see it, the long run always wins in the end. It indubitably limits both the freedom of the individual and even the role of chance.

This approach has won for Braudel an unmatched international reputation. He is widely claimed to be one of the century's great practitioners of his discipline, similarly praised even in Gallic-jealous Britain by conservative historians such as Hugh Trevor-Roper and radicals such as Gareth Stedman Jones. His journal, *Annales*, has been seriously described by some as "the greatest historical journal in the world," and his more enthusiastic academic reviewers have ranked him with Thucydides, Gibbon, Macaulay, and Burckhardt. These accolades have been showered despite the fact that Braudel himself has openly acknowledged that the origins of his approach derived from an experience that was anything but reputable.

Braudel's first major opus began in the 1920s as a graduate thesis on the diplomatic history of Philip II's Mediterranean policy. He says he had the idea for the eventual book, and wrote the first draft of what was to become *The Mediterranean*, while held in a Nazi prisoner of war camp in Lübeck for most of the Second World War. During his "gloomy captivity," he wrote in *Annales* in 1958, he

> struggled a good deal to get away from a chronicle of those difficult years (1940–45). Rejecting events and the time in which events take place was a way of placing oneself to one side, sheltered, so as to get some sort of perspective, to be able to evaluate them better, and not wholly to believe in them.

The event he would have most liked to disbelieve was, of course, the fall of France in 1940. For the Frenchmen of his generation, this event, coupled with the German occupation of Paris without a shot being fired, plus the subsequent collaboration of France with the Nazi regime, was a source of humiliation and anguish.

The concept that most assisted Braudel to distance himself from these events was that of the *"longue durée,"* the structuralist view of history. This is the time span over which he claims the historian can trace the destiny of a civilization, a structure that particular events are powerless to alter, and a broad enough perspective to exonerate men of responsibility for events such as the defeat and occupation of their country. Over the course of the *longue durée*, what did a transient event like the fall of France matter? In *The Identity of France*, Braudel writes that even while the collaborators of the Vichy regime were in power, he believed: "The real France, the France held in reserve, *la France profonde*, remained behind us. It would survive, it did survive . . . Ever since those days, I have never ceased to think of a France buried deep inside itself, within its own heart, a France flowing along the contours of its own age—long history, destined to continue, come what may." In other words, the concept of *la longue durée* has its origins less in a theory of history and more in a peculiarly French combination of nationalist hubris and nostalgia, coupled with shame over their non-performance in the Second World War.

While such an approach might endear him to his countrymen, it obviously does not explain Braudel's success outside France, especially among English-speaking historians whom one would have expected to be the least inclined to support the notion of *la France profonde*. His reputation came largely because he provided a model of how history could be modernized. In the wake of the war, historians were keen to bury the last vestiges of the Victorian emphasis on the heroic individual, especially the chauvinist accounts of imperial heroes like Clive of India or Gordon of Khartoum that had dominated school textbooks as late as the 1930s. Modernization also meant taking on board the work of the fast-growing field of economic history which had found that politics, especially in democratic societies, was more a matter of economic management than had previously been appreciated. Up to the 1960s, anthropology and sociology were still intellectually respectable and some historians felt their own work should be more integrated with these and other social sciences. Braudel showed them how all these aims could be pursued. One of Braudel's most enthusiastic fan clubs was formed by the generation of Marxists who came to prominence in the 1960s, especially in Britain.

While some of the older English Marxist historians, such as Edward Thompson, remained immune, enthusiasm for French ideas raged among Marxist students like a pandemic. Urged on by the most fashionable leftist journal of the day, the London-based *New Left Review*, the generation of Sixties student radicals struggled to incorporate structuralist themes and methods into their theses. Karl Marx himself was something of an ambiguous hero to the editors of *NLR*. Marx, as both historian and revolutionary activist, saw the need to keep some space in his theory for political activism to make a difference to the course of history. His well-known introduction to the *Eighteenth Brumaire of Louis Bonaparte* emphasized the constraints of history and the limitations on free action but stopped short of full-blown determinism. "Men make their own history," he wrote, "but not of their own free will; not under circumstances they themselves have chosen but under the given and inherited circumstances with which they are directly confronted." The academic Left of the 1960s, however, preferred Braudel's insistence on the irrelevance of individual action. An editor of *NLR*, Perry Anderson, wrote *Lineages of the Absolutist State* to press the argument for a determinist approach. By the 1970s his journal was the most ardent advocate of the structuralist brand of Marxism developed by the French Communist Party theorist Louis Althusser. To Althusser, individual men and women have no part in shaping their world. They are merely the bearers of roles that are defined for them by the "social formation," little more than robots programmed by the prevailing capitalist ideology. Though not a Marxist himself, Braudel nonetheless endorsed precisely the theory of history his New Left supporters wanted to hear. "Men do not make history," he wrote in the final passage of *The Identity of France*, "rather it is history above all that makes men and absolves them of blame."

In the wake of the failure of the attempted student revolutionary movement of 1968, and the attendant recall of Charles de Gaulle and election of Richard Nixon, this kind of historical determinism became a comfort blanket for the academic Left. There was no longer any need for a radical to be politically active since activism could make no difference to the great determining structures. All that remained was to study, theorize, and debate the nature of the structures themselves. This was an agenda perfectly suited to the academic world of seminars, conferences, cafés, and bars, and to the careers, tenure, and promotions that have focused their minds ever since.

By the 1980s, the tenured radicals had dropped Marx and Althusser (the latter now an embarrassment since in 1980 he had strangled his seventy-four-year-old wife and been declared insane) but retained their structuralist baggage. Many looked to alternative gurus, notably the former French Marxists Jean Baudrillard and Jean-François Lyotard, who preached postmodernism and spoke of "the end of history." Others turned to Friedrich Nietzsche and the French Nietzschean historian Michel Foucault, who assured them history was no better than a "fictional discourse." "I am well aware," Foucault said, "that I have never written anything but fictions."

There are very few academic historians outside France, however, who are happy about characterizing what they do as writing fiction. Though Foucault still sets much of the agenda for the topics that graduate students research in the 1990s—the study of deviants, criminals, the insane, the sick, and other so-called marginalized minorities—most English-speaking historians are reluctant to openly accept the radical consequences of his views. Nonetheless, since the 1940s, as structuralism and determinism have risen to methodological prominence, a parallel and entirely complementary movement has grown to dominate the debate over the epistemological status of the writing of history. There is a genteel expression of just this point of view in Fernández-Armesto's *Millennium*. "History is a creative art," he says, "best produced with an imagination disciplined by knowledge of and respect for the sources." But he goes on: "To me the test of a good history book is not so much whether the past is verifiably 'reconstructed' and cogently expounded as whether it is convincingly imagined and vividly evoked." Few readers today would question such a declaration. It pays homage to the need for the historian to do more than a novelist and to go out and research the sources. But it also emphasizes, especially through the quotation marks around "reconstructed," that it is not trying to tell what really happened in the past. In short, it is ruling out the notion that the historian can get to the truth of the matter.

There has been a long debate between historians about whether the pursuit of the truth is their ultimate objective. In the nineteenth century, the German historian Leopold von Ranke tried to lay down the methodology for "scientific history," arguing that meticulous pursuit of sources would produce facts that themselves would be the building blocks of conclusions with which the historian could establish the truth about what really happened. Above all, Ranke contended, the historian should avoid imposing his own values, judgments, and biases onto the past he studies. In the last thirty years, Ranke's views have continued to be taught in university courses in historical method, but he has functioned primarily as a straw man to show the folly of the attempt to "reconstruct" the past.

Ranke's critics have argued that he is wrong for three reasons. First, there is no single truth about history to be uncovered. There are many perspectives on the past and we can never encompass them all. Different peoples and eras ask different questions about the past and, just when we think an issue has been settled, a new work can raise a fresh point of view. Second, even the scientific historian has to be selective, to choose some evidence to make his point and to reject others, since he can never attempt to write up everything he finds in his research, let alone everything that happened in the period he is covering. So there must be values or bias built into everything he writes. Third, those academics who have written in the Rankean mold are notorious for being boring and soporific. Their focus on getting their facts meticulously right has been at the expense of recreating the grand sweep of the movement of history that less fussy, more literary writers like Gibbon, Macaulay, and Michelet managed to achieve.

It would not be difficult for most readers of academic history texts to concede, indeed, to strongly endorse, the last of these points, though with all due respect to M. Braudel's lofty reputation, his own work, so devoid of personalities with whom the reader can identify or focus upon, surely ranks as among the most boring of them all. The other two critiques, however, have become so familiar they deserve more consideration. The Dutch historian Peter Geyl emerged in the postwar academic world as one of the most widely read commentators on the discipline. In particular, his books *Napoleon: For and Against* (1949) and *Debates with Historians* (1955) were influential in establishing in the postwar mind the notion that there could be no final truths in history. On Napoleon, he argued, history could "reach no unchallengeable conclusions on so many sided a character." Moreover, "to expect from history those final conclusions which may perhaps be obtained in other disciplines is to misunderstand its nature." Examining the way Napoleon had been represented by historians over the previous century, Geyl argued that different periods sought out and found their own facts and made their own judgments. He argued that this process would always occur and so each generation would always write its own history from the perspective of the political and intellectual environment of its own time and place. Geyl extended this relativist position even to the Germans who had interned him in Buchenwald during the war. He was critical of attempts by historians in the 1950s to trace the origins and pioneers of National Socialism:

> If we are tempted by our horror at the culmination of evil that we have just experienced or witnessed to pick out in the past of Germany all the evil potentialities, we may construct an impressively cogent concatenation of causes and effects leading straight up to that crisis. But the impressiveness and the straightness will be of our own constructing. What we are really doing is to interpret the past in the terms of our own fleeting moment.

Geyl is here discussing not Nazism itself but its possible causes. He remains certain that the Nazi phenomenon itself was "evil." Little did he suspect that his own relativist argument would one day be used to question that very assessment.

In 1961, Geyl's book on Napoleon was favorably acknowledged by the English historian E. H. Carr, author of *What Is History?*, one of the most influential commentaries on history writing ever published. It was a required text in virtually every course on historical method in the English-speaking academic world for the next twenty years. There would be very few of the current generation of practicing historians who have not read it. Carr repeats Geyl's argument that history is "an unending dialogue between the present and the past." Different ages take different perspectives. The best we can hope for is a continuous debate. While he says that historians should base their writing on facts, the real stuff of history is not truth but interpretation. On any topic, he argues, there are an infinite number of facts from which the historian selects. "By and large," Carr says, "the historian will get the kind of facts he wants. History means interpretation." He went on: "If standing Sir George Clark on his head, I were to call history 'a hard core of interpretation surrounded by a pulp of disputable facts', my statement would, no doubt, be one-sided and misleading, but no more so, I venture to think, than the original dictum."

Carr was the author of a massive ten-volume study of the foundation of the USSR between 1917 and 1929 but, until his death in 1982, had remained a closet Marxist. He was only outed in 1987 by the editor of a revised edition of his book on method. His Marxism, however, was of the Old Left variety, and he saw some room for the individual to influence the course of history. In his oft-cited discussion of "society and the individual" in *What Is History?*, Carr says the ability to change history was confined to a highly select few, namely revolutionaries like Cromwell and Lenin who, he says, "helped mould the forces which carried them to greatness." Lesser mortals, even those as powerful as Napoleon and Bismarck, only "rode to greatness on the back of already existing forces." Despite this minor concession to the prospect that men might make their own history, Carr's legacy was to shore up both sides of the emerging consensus about the nature of the discipline. On the one hand, he gave barely qualified support to the structuralist notion that underlying forces were driving the historical process; on the other hand, he became the most eloquent spokesman for the relativist position that each generation, indeed any group of people with a unified perspective, could produce their own version of what they found in the past.

This legacy is alive and well today, not only in grand surveys like that of Fernández-Armesto, but in the common, day-to-day discussion and debate that goes on within the discipline, even among those with no connection to the politics that Carr spent his life supporting. One of the consequences of the relativist position is that it cedes some degree of credibility to anyone with an even vaguely coherent perspective, no matter how vile it might be. This is precisely what is happening today in debate about the Holocaust of the Second World War. A combination of neo-Nazi sympathizers and anti-Semitic skeptics are now claiming either that there was no deliberate plan to exterminate the Jews or else that the number of deaths and the German responsibility for them have been greatly exaggerated. This has reached the stage where Professor Deborah Lipstadt has felt compelled to write *Denying the Holocaust* to rebut the claims. The problem for historians who accept the epistemology of Geyl and Carr is that they lack any firm ground upon which to stand to undertake the same job.

In *The New York Review of Books* of September 19, 1996, there is a review by Gordon A. Craig of a new book on Joseph Goebbels by the English Nazi sympathizer and Holocaust denier David Irving. Craig wrote:

> It is always difficult for the non-historian to remember that there is nothing absolute about historical truth. What we consider as such is only an estimation, based upon what the best available evidence tells us. It must constantly be tested against new information and new interpretations, however implausible they may be, or else it will lose its vitality and degenerate into dogma or shibboleth. Such people as David Irving, then, have an indispensable part in the historical enterprise, and we dare not disregard their views.

Now, Gordon Craig is a well-respected historian of modern Germany, a former president of the American Historical Association and no supporter of the line on the Holocaust pushed by Irving and his ilk. After the above opening, Craig's *NYRB* article goes on to argue against much of the interpretation offered by Irving's book. However, someone operating with Craig's epistemology—history produces no absolute truths—is in a very weak position to do this. He cannot *refute* Irving. The best he can do is *dispute* him. The consequence of the position that there can be no absolute truths is that there can be no absolute falsehoods either, so refutation ("prove the falsehood of") is beyond reach. Craig may well be able to deploy many effective arguments against Irving but, while he retains his epistemological position, he leaves his opponent and all the other Holocaust deniers a window of credibility.

Yet there is no need to concede them this status at all. Far from being impossible, historical truth is not a difficult concept, especially with an issue as recent and as well-recorded as the Holocaust. The sources for the vast majority of independent evidence we have about this event—perpetrators as well as victims, survivors, and witnesses—corroborate each other. For every corroboration, there increases in geometric proportion the probability that this event actually occurred. Since we live in a finite world, there comes a point where it is impossible for any scenario to exist in which the Holocaust did not occur. This remains true no matter how many particular or less generalized aspects of the event—the total numbers involved, whether Hitler personally ordered it, etc.—remain uncertain. The proposition that the event known as the Holocaust took place is an absolute historical truth. Let me give a different example to underline this point. Another contender for historical truth might be the proposition: "The United States defeated Japan in the Second World War." Now this is something that we know not simply from the historical record. It is no mere interpretation derived from an examination of the documents of surrender signed aboard the U.S.S. *Missouri* in Tokyo Harbor in 1945. It is not an interpretation that future generations might overturn after they have scoured the nuances of the texts for so far undiscerned ideological meaning. The fact that the United States defeated Japan has shaped the very world that all of us have inhabited since 1945. The relations between states, the world economy, the employment market of every industrial country are all consequences in various ways of this historical truth. The world itself confirms the proposition.

Of course, E. H. Carr might argue the defeat of Japan is a mere "fact" and the really interesting discussions are the interpretations historians make and the conclusions they draw from facts of this kind. Well, one man's fact can be another man's conclusion. For someone writing a narrative history of the war in the Pacific, the defeat of Japan is a very big conclusion indeed. There is no event that is inherently confined to the status of a mere fact, that is, a building block of a much larger conclusion. Every fact can itself be a conclusion and every conclusion can itself be a fact in someone else's explanation.

All this is not to argue that history has to be confined forever, in a Rankean sense, only to facts that have been conclusively proven to be true. History is not only a science, it is an art and, moreover, it often deals in value judgments. Historians frequently offer interpretations that they know, because of the limitations of the available evidence, will forever remain interpretations and bones of contention. There are some historical questions that will probably never be answered to everyone's satisfaction—the causes of the industrial revolution in Britain, for instance, is a likely recent contender. Many of these latter questions, it should be openly admitted, are among the most interesting interrogations we can make of the past. But the existence of uncertainty and the necessity of value judgments, even on a wide scale, remain perfectly compatible with our ability to establish certainty in some, indeed a great many, cases. The argument from Peter Geyl—some historical interpretations are transient, therefore all historical findings are questionable, therefore history is necessarily unreliable—is nothing more than an invalid inference. When one of its consequences is the irrefutability of a Nazi sympathizer's denial of the Holocaust, decency as well as logic demands that it now be abandoned. In defending the ability of historians to get to the truth of the matter, or at least of some matters, I am referring to the traditional, empirically grounded practice of historians rather than to those speculative works that claim to find some great underlying force—be it geography, ideology, or the imperative of the class struggle—driving the historical process. History is an invention of Western culture, dating from ancient Greece in the fifth century B.C., and since then its practice has been confined almost entirely to the West. No other culture has produced, or been able to live with, the notion that it is possible to examine the passage of social affairs in a way that is independent of both the prevailing religion and the prevailing political system.

Yet for much of this time, there have been two traditions of history contesting the field. One derives from the first genuine historian, Thucydides. Other ancient Greek works of his era have used the term "history," but it was Thucydides in *History of the Peloponnesian War*, written some time between 424 and 400 B.C., who rejected reliance on sacred texts, myth, legend, and rumor and adopted a strictly empirical research method. "Of the events of war," he wrote, "I have not ventured to speak from any chance information, nor according to any notion of my own. I have described nothing but what I saw myself, or learned from others of whom I made the most careful and particular enquiry." That other pillar of Western culture, the Judeo-Christian tradition, played an essential role in preserving and nourishing the historiographic impulse. In the *Oxford Illustrated History of Christianity* (1990), John Mc-Manners has argued that in the implications of Christian belief there are encouragements to writing history in an austere, uncommitted fashion, with wide cultural concern:

> Firstly, there was the conviction that everything men do or think matters intensely and eternally, as coming under the judgement of God; secondly, there was the concept of a creator entirely distinct from his creation, ruling the universe by general laws, whose ways are inscrutable, and who gives men the gift of freedom. Hence the obligation to treat seriously and with reverence all men and the social orders they build, to study everything, to explain without partisanship, insisting on the logical coherence of all things.

From the fall of Rome to the Renaissance, the idea of history was kept alive in the industry of those many Christian monks whose chronicles of church and state were imbued with ideals of this kind.

Christianity, however, bore an additional dimension that in the last two centuries has produced a second tradition within history. Christianity has held that, while the achievements of man are due to his own will and intellect, they are also beholden to something other than himself, the realizing of God's purposes for man. From this perspective, men are the vehicles through which history occurs but history has a direction and a purpose decided by a force beyond man. This Christian concept of history also contained the idea of fulfillment. The purpose of history would one day be realized in the salvation of mankind at the Last Judgment. History is thus a teleological process with a purpose and an end. It is this second aspect of the Christian tradition that has formed the basis of those theories of history that conjure up great impersonal forces and undercurrents which purportedly determine the destiny of mankind.

At the turn of the nineteenth century, the German philosopher Georg Wilhelm Friedrich Hegel secularized the theory, substituting "reason" for God's will. The object of history for Hegel was the realization of reason's purpose of creating a just and free society. Hegel thought this had occurred at the Battle of Jena in 1806 when Napoleon defeated the *ancien régime* of Germany and cleared the way for the establishment of the French revolutionary principles of liberty and equality. Forty years later, Karl Marx modified Hegel to argue that the underlying force of history was the class struggle, which was driving human society to ever higher stages of development, of which the final plane would be Communist society.

Given the track record of Hegel and Marx and the manifest failure of both to correctly identify anything remotely resembling the fulfillment of history, the teleological aspect of their approach is, not surprisingly, out of favor in the late twentieth century. Only the more loony postmodernists like Jean Baudrillard and the lone Hegelian voice of Francis Fukuyama talk about the "end of history" today. But there are still plenty of theorists who support an otherwise very similar "great impersonal forces" approach. Fernand Braudel and his imitators like Felipe Fernández-Armesto are merely the latest in this same tradition, only with one important difference. The Christian theologians such as St. Augustine who developed the original version knew that it depended on a powerful force to act as the engine of history, in their case God. Hegel and Marx recognized something similar. Though their concepts of reason and class struggle were secular, and generated from within mankind itself, they still functioned as theoretical engines, driving everything along and bringing new stages of history into being. But the Braudel brand of structuralism has no such driving force. Geography, climate, and topography do not constitute great underlying currents for mankind. All they can possibly be are part of the external framework within which events occur. At most, they might place some limitations on human action. But by no stretch of the metaphorical imagination can geography ever be said to be responsible for the "destiny" and the "fate" of mankind, as Braudel claims. His concept of destiny and fate requires some kind of powerful causative agent that can defy the best effort of mankind's will and intellect, and can bend human outcomes to its purpose. In the *Annales* school and the other varieties of French structuralism, such an agent is precisely what is missing.

All such theories about "underlying forces" also fall prey to the old logical positivist critique of metaphysics. The forces are taken as given; people shaped by them are unaware of their presence; they can only be detected by the imagination of a great scholar taking a long view of things. Their existence is not dependent upon any evidence that can be verified or falsified; or rather, if there is evidence that appears to question them it is the evidence that needs to be explained away, not the forces. To believe in phenomena like the "cunning of reason," the class struggle, or *la longue durée* is to take a leap of faith. It is to treat works of history that endorse them not as the products of evidence and reason but as sacred texts, handed down by authority and to be learned but not questioned by the faithful.

One of the reasons for the esteem the *Annales* school enjoyed in France in the postwar period was that it not only relegated the fall of France to the status of a minor eddy in the grand stream of French history, but it did the same to the Revolution of 1789. From the fall of Napoleon to the end of the Third Republic, French society and politics had been racked by division over the Revolution. One of the major polarizations of the 1930s was between supporters of the "revolutionaries" and those of the "counterrevolutionaries." After the war, this debilitating conflict was widely identified as one of the causes of France's defeat. It was not surprising, then, that a movement bent on relegating political history to a position of small importance would be welcomed as a means of fostering national harmony. By the 1980s, however, the consequences were causing alarm among French political leaders, especially after a 1983 survey found that only one-third of children entering secondary school could give the date of the French Revolution. While some English-speaking countries might regard this as a comparatively high rate of political awareness, French President François Mitterand declared the "deficiency of teaching history" to be "a national danger."

In her 1987 collection of essays, *The New History and the Old*, the American historian Gertrude Himmelfarb noted Mitterand's concern and observed that similar tendencies had been evident in the U.S. education system ever since social history, "total history," and "history from below" had come to dominate the curriculum at the expense of political history. She argues that balance needs to be restored, especially since political history is an exercise in two kinds of human reason: that reflected in the rational ordering of society by means of laws, constitutions, and political institutions, and that of the rational activity of the historian seeking to discover and to transmit the truth about society. Himmelfarb's essays constitute the most eloquent and persuasive recent defense of the first of the Western historical traditions described above, that deriving from Thucydides and the medieval monastic chroniclers. Rather than human affairs being impelled by great impersonal forces, political history reveals our world to be made by men and, instead of being "absolved of blame," men are responsible for the consequences of their actions. This was the very point that informed Thucydides' study of the Peloponnesian War: the fate of Athens had been determined not by prophets, oracles, or the gods, but by human actions and social organization. Himmelfarb says good history demonstrates Aristotle's claim that "man is by nature a political animal." It is not in the "household" or the "village" but only in the "polis," Aristotle said, that man is truly human and decisively different from other gregarious animals. What these animals lack is a polity, "a government of laws and institutions by means of which—and only by means of which, Aristotle believed—man consciously, rationally tries to establish a just regime and pursue the good life."

Hence, the demise of political history in recent decades and the rise of the various impersonal theories that deny men are agents of their own fate lead not only to the kind of bizarre judgment that would make China rather than

Western Europe and its offshoots the leading force of this past millennium. It also involves, Himmelfarb argues, a radical redefinition of human nature, by which we

> lose not only the unifying theme that has given coherence to history, not only the notable events, individuals and institutions that have constituted our historical memory and our heritage, not only the narrative that has made history readable and memorable—not only, in short, a meaningful past—but also a conception of man as a rational, political animal.

Himmelfarb wisely observes that orthodoxies usually breed heretics. This is true, but the nonconformists who today see the need for a reformation to restore the traditional practice of history remain a minority in terms of both numbers and reputation. With this in mind, and with little optimism about any rapid reversal of the status quo, let me finish by advocating a course of action suggested by one of the theologians of the present orthodoxy, Peter Geyl. In the days when his own views appeared a tantalizing heresy, he got at least one thing right: "Criticism is the first duty of historical scholarship," he declared, "criticism, again criticism, and criticism once more."

March 1997

Present-Tense Culture

Mark Steyn

A YEAR or two back, my small town in New Hampshire completed the decades-long process of educational "consolidation" and closed our last one-room schoolhouse—a fine 1839 clapboard academy atop a hill overlooking a small settlement. For the last thirty years, it had been used as the town kindergarten, but now the little ones have gone downhill to join their siblings in the first-to-eighth grade school. The town isn't sure yet what to do with the building, so the classroom's been tidied up and decorated with some surviving artifacts of its illustrious past. On the blackboard is a typical math exercise of the mid-nineteenth century: "If 46 yards of cloth cost £53 10s 6d, what is that per yard?" The tattered volume from which it's taken sits on a pupil's desk three rows back, with the names of several of the town's oldest families inscribed inside. It's an American book published in 1855—a time when children were required to do compound division not only in their own decimal currency but in the more awkward coinage of distant lands.

I wonder how many elementary school pupils today could answer that question? I wonder how many of their teachers could? I wonder how many would be able to tell you what "sterling" was and of which country it was the currency? If you object that, in an age of computers and calculators, nobody needs to be able to do long division, the vast army of Americans mortgaged to the hilt and drowning in credit-card debt suggests otherwise. We don't buy yards of cloth so much, but how about "If North Country Chevrolet offers you a two-year lease for twenty-four thousand miles at $299 per month with $750 down, how much are you paying per mile (Vermont residents add sales tax)?" or "If MCI calls up and offers you a calling plan of 12¢ per minute off peak . . . ?"

A few miles down the road from our abandoned academy is our triumphantly consolidated elementary school. You know when you're getting near because a sign tells you, as it does in every town in the state, that you're now entering a "Drug-Free School Zone." I loathe that sign not because of any drug danger, real or perceived, but because of the priorities it implies: it seems the best we can hope for from a public education system is that our children aren't heroin dealers by the time they've been through it. But why stop there? Why not "You Are Now Entering a Latin-Free School Zone"? That, at least, is beyond dispute.

In England and Wales, according to a recent survey, pre-Romantic poetry has almost vanished from the classrooms—not because the pupils can't understand it, but because the teachers can't. Pope? Milton? Marvell and his "Coy Mistress"? Love to help you, mate, but I can't make head or tail of it. On the other hand, an inability to understand the language is no obstacle to being able to "empathize" with previous generations. "Empathy" is what passes for history in most British and North American schools these days: you'll be asked to "empathize" with a West African who is sold into slavery and shipped off to the British West Indies, or with a hapless Native American who catches dysentery, typhoid, gonorrhea, a heavy cold, and an early strain of HIV by foolishly buying beads from Christopher Columbus.

The exercise would be worthwhile if we genuinely "empathized" with them: the Indian might be motivated by greed or lust or fury, the black slave might be fatalistic, optimistic, indifferent. But that's not what educational "empathy" is about: instead we're supposed to assign the slave a contemporary African-American identity and thereby understand his sense of injustice; we're supposed to acknowledge the Native American as the first victim of European racism. It seems the Indians never scalped anyone, unless you count the mass frontal lobotomy they've metaphorically performed on the teachers' unions. This is the very opposite of "empathy"; it's the projection of our drearily limited obsessions—racism, sexism, imperialism, homophobia—over the rich canvas of the past. That's the thing about "diversity" and "multiculturalism": they lead, paradoxically but remorselessly, to homogeneity and parochialism.

Funnily enough, across the corridor in the English classroom, the teacher is less happy to trust to our "empathy." As a child, I read all kinds of books, good and bad: *Tom Sawyer* and *Tom Brown*, *Treasure Island* and C. S. Lewis, Sir Walter Scott and *Anne of Green Gables* . . . I had no idea that these books were not "relevant" to me. I was aware that most of these children lived lives that differed from mine to one degree or another—in Enid Blyton, the "Famous Five" exist on a diet of ginger beer and veal-ham-and-egg pie, neither of which I'd experienced. But it never occurred to me that such details were preventing me from "relating" to these stories. A child has no very precise sense of time, of anachronisms, of obsolescence, of whether his adventures are set in the 1950s or 1920s or 1700s—or what those designations mean: his imagination soars free of such considerations. Back in small-town New Hampshire, when the Congregational Church celebrated its bicentenary, a little boy, impressed by the pageant, said to the elderly lady who'd organized it, "Wow! You mean you do this every 200 years?"

There will be time enough later on to fence ourselves in with superficial prejudices and define ourselves generationally: baby boomers or Gen Xers, disco or grunge, "Brady Bunch" or "Beavis and Butt-head" . . . In those first formative years, a child's mind is untrammeled: he or she doesn't notice that Huck Finn and Heidi are "out of date"; the concept, at that age, is meaningless. It's only a problem for our educators, projecting onto their charges the same misbegotten "empathy" they tout for America's victim classes.

Wander into the children's section of the bookstore and pluck at random. Jacket copy for Lois Ruby's *Skin Deep*: "Dan was her best friend, her boyfriend, a good guy. He'd always been a little withdrawn, but he never seemed like the type to hate people for the color of their skin. Or for what they believed. Laurel soon realizes that Dan's in too deep. That her boyfriend has become a neo-Nazi skinhead." Or John Neufeld's *Almost a Hero*: "Ben is convinced his spring vacation has been ruined by his social studies teacher's assignment—a week's volunteer service for a community charity. Haunted by something dark in his own past, Ben chooses to work at Sidewalk's End, a day care center for homeless children. When Ben believes he sees Batista, one of the Sidewalk's End kids, being abused by his mother at a grocery store, he is frustrated by his inability to get the authorities to act to protect the child."

These two approaches—false "empathy" and bogus "relevance"—were not cooked up by the public schools in isolation; they run right through contemporary culture. What is Demi Moore's version of *The Scarlet Letter* but an especially severe case of misplaced "empathy"? The past is history. That's to say, it's history in the sense of that robust and revealing American formulation: "Bob Dole? Aw, he's history!"—as in fuhgeddabout him, he's through, he's washed up, he don't mean diddlysquat, he won't trouble us no more, we need pay him no further heed. He's history.

It's a superb phrase, awesome in its contempt, exhaustive in its concision, and a fine catchphrase for the times. If a living culture has traditionally been a dialogue between the present and the past, then today one side has fallen silent—or, at any rate, been drowned out. In the din of the present—the bass line of the CD thudding from the apartment downstairs, the TV flickering away in front of the bored gas station clerk, the bleep-bleep-bleep of the video arcade—our ancestral voices have a harder time than ever making their presence felt. When was the last time you heard a politician quote a Greek or a Roman, or anybody before Churchill? In 1940, Leo Amery, speaking in the House of Commons after the fall of France, rebuked Neville Chamberlain and his colleagues thus:

> I will quote certain other words. I do it with great reluctance, because I am speaking of those who are old friends and associates of mine, but they are words which, I think, are applicable to the present situation. This is what Cromwell said to the Long Parliament when he thought it was no longer fit to conduct the affairs of the nation: "You have sat too long here for any good you have been doing. Depart, I say, and let us have done with you. In the name of God, go."

Maybe someone should try that with President Clinton. Then again, maybe it's too long for a soundbite. There was pop culture in 1940, even within the Palace of Westminster: the MP A. P. Herbert was a successful humorist and lyricist and the author of the popular song "Other People's Babies." Across the Atlantic, there was *Pal Joey* and Major Bowes, Superman and *Fantasia*, Jack Benny and the Andrews Sisters—and a new hamburger restaurant started by a couple of Pasadena movie-theater owners, Richard and Maurice McDonald. But, in those days, pop culture was not the only vernacular in which the business of the nation was translated.

A present-tense culture is bound to be narcissistic, but, even so, its impregnability is impressive. Recently, Reebok was startled to be attacked by various women's groups for launching a new brand of footwear called "Incubus." It's not necessary to subscribe to the feminist argument that an incubus is a sort of prototype Clarence Thomas to wonder why, having spent a fortune on market research and focus groups and target testing, Reebok couldn't have given some intern fifteen bucks to go around the corner and buy a dictionary. Although most commentators described it as a Latin word, it's in my *Pocket Oxford*, quaintly considered part of the English language, albeit in the early pre-Ebonics phase of its development:

> INCUBUS *n.* oppressive person or thing; evil spirit visiting sleeper.

No doubt one day the company will unveil the Reebok Gulag: the word tested well with the focus groups, who agreed it evoked the sophisticated Continental chic they look for in a running shoe. Each night, it seems, the evil spirit steals upon our sleeping form and sucks away a little bit more of what we once took for granted.

Shortly after the basketball player Magic Johnson announced he was HIV positive, an "AIDS educator" appeared on the TV news and declared that her organization had been overwhelmed by callers anxious for information on "safe sex." Johnson's disclosure had so raised the public profile of the pandemic, she said, that to her and her co-workers it had become a kind of dividing line: A.M. and P.M. As she explained helpfully, A.M. stood for After Magic, P.M. for Pre-Magic. You might have expected *someone* in the office to say, "Hang on, in the normal course of the day doesn't P.M. come *after* A.M.? D'you think there's any reason for that?" I learned about ante meridiem and post meridiem at the age of seven, when, in an introduction to the classics, our teacher drew our attention to Latin phrases in everyday use. Until that news bulletin, it had never occurred to me that for others it might be the sort of rarefied arcana you'd have to do a BA in to ever stumble across.

In deference to that "educator," I think we should call this condition PMS—Post-Media Solipsism. The information superhighway seems to be a kind of giant rotary in which we go round and round colliding only with the other flotsam and jetsam of the here and now. For the most advanced case, look no further than the president during the 1996 campaign: "The last time I checked, the Constitution said, 'Of the people, by the people and for the people.' That's what the Declaration of Independence says."

Well, of course, he didn't check. He doesn't have to. The Declaration of Independence or the Gettysburg Address? What's the diff? Abe Lincoln? He's history. Indeed, the fate of Bob Dole's presidential candidacy, built on his poor doomed offer to be "the bridge to that better past," is instructive. When President Clinton, hijacking his opponent's metaphor, reconstructed it as "the bridge to the twenty-first century," he and his triangulating pollsters understood that a modern, electronic culture exists in a state of perpetual anticipation: even as the credits of your favorite sitcom start to roll, the screen consigns them to a tiny corner and a trailer commends the delights of the next, even funnier sitcom—or, as they say before the breaks on "Entertainment Tonight," the celebrity gossip magazine which so seamlessly follows the network news in most American cities, "Coming up! A minor character in a soap opera shoots her new swimsuit calendar—and ET has an exclusive preview!" (I quote from memory.) No matter that the item, by the time it arrives, seems barely longer than the clips and promos and teasers that have preceded it: by then something else will be coming up. When we reach that bridge to the twenty-first century, we'll be sitting in gridlock with the same old crack users, gangsta rappers, Indonesian caffeine addicts, and pre-op transsexual Hawaiian honeymooners, but by then the president will have moved on to the "new promise" of a bridge to the twenty-second century, or the fourth millennium, or a week next Tuesday—all coming up!

President Clinton is only the most brazenly fatuous co-opter, but these days all "forward-looking" states subscribe to the same philosophy: the past is something to be left behind. The members of the European Union, for example, are committed, by binding treaty, to "an ever closer union": in the end, therefore, efforts by British Conservative Euroskeptics to maintain, say, the United Kingdom's right to sell beer in imperial pints are bound to fail. The uniform metric Euro*stein* can be postponed, but never vanquished: forward momentum is a permanent constitutional condition of the Union. And when can it ever be deemed close enough?

Similarly, my native land, Canada, recently changed the motto on its coat of arms. After the flag, this is the second most visible formal emblem of the nation, embossed on the fronts of our passports and most official documents. Ever since the Dominion of Canada was established in 1867, the motto has read, *"A Mari usque ad Mare"*—from sea to sea. It's now been augmented by *"Desiderantes Meliorem Patriam"*—they desire a better country. Why not go all the way and just say "Canada—A Work in Progress"?

There was no parliamentary debate about the new motto: we just woke up one morning and discovered, thanks to a disgruntled opposition MP, that there it was. Brushing aside pedantic criticisms, the minister responsible said she couldn't see what all the fuss was about: they'd sent the proposed change to the Queen, she'd liked it and had been happy to approve it. This buck-passing was, in its way, even more shameless than the new motto: it's a fundamental constitutional practice in Commonwealth countries that the sovereign doesn't personally endorse the actions done in her name; they're the responsibility of her ministers. The disregard for constitutional proprieties, as much as the discarding of history, tells us much about the "better country" they so desire.

But then uneasy lies the head that wears the crown in a sound-bite culture. In Britain, forced to defend the monarchy from recent self-inflicted embarrassments, Conservative MPs tend to say things like, "Well, it's jolly good value for the money. The Royal Family brings an awful lot of tourism into the country." It's a pop culture response: Princess Di as a dysfunctional Minnie Mouse. But how else to explain it? The thinly veiled republicans on the Labor and Liberal benches tend to propose curtailing the Crown's powers or abolishing the House of Lords because, so they reason, if you were starting today, you'd never do it that way.

That's the point: we don't *need* to start today. The Liberal Party is resentful that the institutions of so many European countries seem more modern than Britain's, but that's because those nation states fail every generation or two and have to start from scratch. The West's successful nations—which broadly speaking are the English-speaking ones—have somehow managed, in defiance of the old countryman's advice, to get here from there. It says much for the degree to which the obsession with novelty has infected every area of life that our institutions' longevity should now be their principal offense. Progressive opinion, for example, has long held that British judges and barristers should abandon their wigs and robes because ordinary members of the public are unnerved by them.

The condescension is exquisite: ordinary members of the public aren't unnerved by Elton John wearing a Versace dress in *The Sunday Times*, or Dennis Rodman and Mayor Giuliani. But surely we aren't such novelty junkies that we don't see the antiquated garb for what it really is: a reassurance—that the justice system predates the fads and fashions of the present day. In the Caribbean, the speakers of those tiny, British-derived island parliaments love their wigs and maces and copies of Hansard: they advertise, in stark contrast to their neighbors in Cuba, Haiti, and the Dominican Republic, their peaceful constitutional evolution. Unlike the American multiculturalists, they see no shame in acknowledging the origins of their institutions.

It's a different story in Canada. On the coat of arms,

above the motto and below the crown, you'll see the English and Scottish lions, the Irish harp and the French fleur-de-lis. These four peoples built the Canadian state, on traditions inherited from home (parliamentary democracy) and institutions constructed on site (the Hudson's Bay Company, the Royal Canadian Mounted Police, the Canadian Pacific Railroad). One day, we'll wake up and they'll be gone, too. The official version of the modern state can be seen on the bus posters advertising the fiftieth anniversary of Canadian citizenship: "Canada—It Means the World to Us," and underneath stand representatives of every conceivable ethnic background holding hands around a globe as if they'd like to teach the world to sing in perfect harmoneeee.

A generation ago, Canada decided to reinvent itself as a round-the-clock Coke commercial, establishing a minister for multiculturalism and a Canadian Consultative Council of Multiculturalism. Many countries adapt and evolve and drift far away from their roots, but Canada, uniquely in the civilized world, simply junked its past. One reason I'm sympathetic to Francophone nationalism is that I think Quebeckers have a point: how can they trust Ottawa to protect French-Canadian culture when Ottawa couldn't even be bothered protecting English-Canadian culture? I happen to be an Irish-Belgian-Canadian, but it's absurd to maintain that the Irish contribution to Canadian history can be ranked no higher than the Belgian contribution. It's difficult even in a dictatorship convincingly to substitute a fiction for history: when its phoniness is self-evident, public cynicism is inevitable. The tragedy for Canada is that, when Quebec does leave, there'll be nothing left: they tore down the old Brittanic Dominion and couldn't find anything to put in its place.

Canada doesn't see it that way, admittedly. Its champions are forever trumpeting this or that United Nations survey showing that it's the best country in the world. The reason, obviously, is that Canada is the country that best approaches the condition of the United Nations. Far away from Canada, those peoples hung up on history are doomed as irredeemably recidivist: if only the Balkans would cease refighting their ancient quarrels; if only those Serb irregulars could be prized free from time-honored traditions like genital severing and just watch rock videos like normal people.

On a recent BBC documentary about Northern Ireland, after some footage of an Orangemen's pipe-and-drum marching band noisily commemorating some or other glorious victory of King Billy, the urbane English commentator remarked laconically, "Some of us wonder why can't the Unionists just pipe down?" If you dropped Belfast and Londonderry in the middle of the United States, they'd be two of the safest cities in the country, with annual murder rates that would tally up to an average weekend in Baton Rouge, Louisiana, or Gary, Indiana. But, because they're killing each other not in drug deals and drive-by shootings, liquor store hold-ups and domestic disputes but rather in an ongoing feud rooted in hundreds of years of history, it's deplored as a terrible tragedy. When President Clinton insists on his commitment to "advance" the peace process in Ulster, the British Government should politely inquire as to the murder rate in his own capital city. But they don't, of course: they, too, are wedded to their "initiatives," creatures of a culture where everything is always in play, up for grabs.

This idea of the nation as an ongoing one-way street is a curious one. To be sure, our most enduring stories are of epic journeys into the unknown, but they also involve returning to the certainties of home—not just in Homer (well named), but also in *The Lord of the Rings*, which several recent British literary surveys are touting as "the book of the century." To take a comparable American fable, for Dorothy the point of following the Yellow Brick Road was to get back to Kansas. Last November, Bob Dole wanted to get back to Kansas, while Bill Clinton believed we should follow the Yellow Brick Road for no other reason than that it leads away from where we are now. As the poet Thom Gunn wrote, shortly before moving from Britain to America, "You're always nearer by not keeping still."

The question is: nearer to *what*? It's not so much that the pace of change is constantly accelerating as that change itself has changed. In the first half of this century, the pattern of our days altered drastically: we began to move about by cars, and airplanes, and to converse by telephone; the invention of the elevator spurred the invention of the skyscraper; electric lighting and refrigerators made the old lamp-lighter and the iceman redundant; self-raising flour and washing machines helped eliminate the need for domestic servants; the outhouse moved indoors. A young man, propelled by an H. G. Wells time machine from 1897 to 1947, would be flummoxed at every turn. By contrast, a young man, catapulted from 1947 to 1997, would, on the surface, feel instantly at home. In the second half of the century, hardly anything has changed: our bathrooms, our washers, our kitchens, our high-rises, our cars and planes have barely altered.

But, after a while, the young man from 1947 would begin to notice a few differences—not technological so much as psychological. Of a mind to take in a show or a movie, he might pick up *The Village Voice* or *The Boston Phoenix* and find himself confronted with pages of ads for unspecified services available by calling 1-900-287-SLUT, 1-800-890-TITS, or 1-800-333-ANAL. Even more than the fact that such services are freely—or rather expensively—available, he might be surprised to find himself in a world where, when a prospective customer calls the telephone company to set up a phone line or two and the service representative asks was there any particular number you had in mind and the customer inquires whether 1-888-GAY-REAR is still available, the phone company—the heirs of Alexander Graham Bell—says "1-888-GAY-REAR? No problem. It's yours, sir." (The numbers quoted are all real, so, if you dial them up, make sure you have a credit card handy.) Every invention has unintended consequences, but it's hard to avoid the suspicion that, after a century of continuous mechanization, the unintended consequences are the only ones left; the touch-tone phone has had a few peripheral benefits, but its principal effect, like that of so many others, is to nudge us further down the road to social isolation.

The argument in favor of these novelties is usually a First Amendment one—that America's Founding Fathers had cannily foreseen the inventions of phone sex and gangsta rap and took great care to bequeath us their post-humous endorsement. The discovery of these and other latent rights is the constitutional equivalent of "If Shakespeare were alive today, he'd be writing 'Baywatch'": it depends on the theory of continuous forward propulsion, and the assumption that there are no absolutes, no standards; there can be no lines drawn in the sands of time. If you venture unease about Snoop Doggy Dogg singing "Don't muthafuck with me, you muthafucker," you'll be told that ah, yes, but once upon a time the waltz was considered shocking.

When C. Delores Tucker and William Bennett met with Time Warner to protest the company's involvement in gangsta rap, one executive responded, "Elvis was more controversial in his day than some rap lyrics are today." In a way, that's even more alarming—for it presupposes that pretty soon we'll get used to Snoop and 2Pac and the Notorious B.I.G. and that one day at the Elks' or the Legion hall we'll raise a glass to Irv and Mildred's fiftieth anniversary and they'll whirl out on the floor as the band plays that old favorite they used to dance to when they were courting: "Yo, Bitch! Sit on This." And we'll all sigh, "Ah, why don't they write 'em like they used to?" and moan about what the kids are listening to today. If in forty years we've gone from Elvis to the Dogg, where will we be in another forty years, or even twenty?

Throughout this century, American innovation has been brash and raucous—as it was (though it's hard to believe) in the British Empire at its zenith. But, underneath the noise, there were certain assumptions. In 1934, for example, there was a pop hit called "Love Is Just around the Corner," whose middle section ran:

Venus de Milo
Was noted for her charms
Strictly between us
You're cuter than Venus
And what's more you've got arms.

This isn't some chichi showtune; it was a big song in a popular movie and it became a best-selling record for Bing Crosby. Its authors, Ralph Rainger and Leo Robin, are unknown outside the songwriting community. But, back in 1934, Robin could make mention in a pop song of the Venus de Milo and he and his publisher and the movie's producer could all be confident that, somewhere at the back of their minds, most listeners would have a hazy image of a statue with its arms missing.

Songs and jokes are our common currency, the most reliable guide to what it is we share. Not so long ago, a vaudevillian, reacting to a novelty song that had fallen a little flat, could chide his audience, "I see that you have Van Gogh's ear for music"; a TV variety show would include a sketch that ran: "Coming to the pub, Franz Schubert?" "Not tonight, I have to stay in and finish my symphony," etc. You can find a thousand similar references in the popular culture of sixty years ago, but not now. These aren't the deliberately obscure allusions to William Burroughs buried on 1960s concept albums, but a kind of casual cultural vocabulary that assumes that someone who digs swing bands and gangster movies can be relied upon to have a certain elementary recognition of the "classics" —great novels and old masters and classical music: the "canon" extended even unto Crosby lyrics.

True, there were those who had forgotten or never learned what the Venus de Milo or Schubert's "Unfinished" Symphony was, but they tended to feel sheepish about such lapses. You rarely came across fellows like the Hispanic rapper being interviewed on TV a year or two back who claimed that he didn't want to learn 'bout no George Washington 'cuz George Washington had no relevance to him. As it happens, I'm not ill-disposed toward Hispanic rap, taking the view that rap, like opera, tends to be most agreeable in a language one doesn't understand. But someone should point out to the chap that George

Washington and a few other dead white males of no relevance are the reasons that he finds it more congenial to pursue his calling as a Hispanic rapper in Los Angeles rather than Guatemala City. Still, why blame him when the Federal government itself is happy to wipe the birthdays of Washington and Lincoln off the calendar and merge them into that big nothing, Presidents' Day? Washington? He's history.

By such criteria, very little history is "relevant." Today, the word "classics" is applied not to Greek and Latin but to early Stones cuts or some newly discovered digitally remastered episodes of "The Beverly Hillbillies." In lieu of real, living history, it's possible to live in ersatz history twenty-four hours a day, tuned to finely targeted radio stations offering round-the-clock hits from, according to taste, the Sixties, Seventies, Eighties, or even the late Seventies/early Eighties—part of the virtual ghettos that have risen up instead of the dreaming spires of Marshall McLuhan's promised global village.

Traditional societies appear like icebergs: beneath the surface, there's the unseen seven-eighths, the shared history on which the top eighth sits. When William Mann of the London *Times* became the first critic to write seriously about The Beatles, he did so by banging on about "aeolian cadences" and similar terms. He felt that, if you were going to argue the musical merits of the Fab Four, you had to submit them to the same technical analysis as you would Schubert. For his pains, John Lennon dismissed Mann as a "bullshitter." Offering an alternative explanation, Paul McCartney said, "There are always two things we do when we sit down to write a song. First we sit down. Then we write a song."

Thirty years later, the Mann model has all but vanished. A critic or a professor—for these things are now the province of the academy—cannot (as Wilfred Mellers once did) compare The Beatles with Schubert, because he has no very clear idea of what Schubert did. Mann's successor in the *Times*, David Sinclair, writes of the trio Rapeman:

> Albini favors a thin, scratchy guitar sound, massively over-cranked to deliver squalls of feedback . . . Solos unfold like so much sonic splatter. . . . Albini's singing is a rabidly incoherent, hysterical shriek that brings a number of the songs to the verge of self-destruction.

In case you haven't twigged, Sinclair's giving the boys a rave. One can only admire, he decides, Rapeman's "high degree of individual musicianship," not to mention "the scalpel-sharp sense of purpose to which it is harnessed." For Mann, if The Beatles merited a place in the canon, they had to submit to the same admission criteria as Brahms or Wolf. For Mann's successors, rock criticism is arguably one of the most seminal things since the last arguably seminal thing a couple of days ago.

The London *Times*, like *The New York Times* and most other papers, has exhaustive coverage of rock music, but very little of it has to do with "aeolian cadences." The bottom seven-eighths of the iceberg has melted away and what's left bobs around on the water alluding only to itself —rock 'n' movies 'n' Calvin Klein ads 'n' junk food 'n' Clinton jokes . . . Moreover, in this present-tense culture, the occasional forays down the highbrow end are even more unconvincing than Mellers and Mann were. When Henry Louis Gates, Jr., Harvard Professor of English and Afro-American Studies, was called as an expert witness in the obscenity trial of 2 Live Crew, he cited, as an example of the respectable poetic tradition of explicit sexual imagery, "Shakespeare's 'My Love is like a red, red rose.'" No reporter, even assuming he'd spotted it, was tactless enough to mention that the Professor's quoted line comes not from the Bard but Robbie Burns. But who cares? "A rose is a rose is a rose," as Gertrude Lawrence famously said. Robbie Burns? He's history.

Across the swamp of our know-nothing culture, the Harvard professor reaches lazily out to the Hispanic rapper, wallowing in the mud like two dozey hippos. All of our ancient institutions are vulnerable in a media age: when everything is brand-new, up-to-the-minute or, at any rate, all-improved and excitingly relaunched, what's the point of anything whose authority derives from the fact that it was around before you were born? For the Royal Family, the solution was to tiptoe gingerly into the shallow end of modern celebrity: Their Royal Highnesses the Duke and Duchess of York and the Prince Edward agreed to be team captains on a Royal game show; a decade later, Prince Edward is a TV producer, the Duchess does commercials for Ocean Spray cranberry juice, and the Duke spends much of his time denying he has AIDS.

For the Church of England, the solution was to try to get a bit more with-it, daddy-o: the Bishop of Durham, apparently a born-again doubter, described the Resurrection as "basically a sort of conjuring trick with bones"; less elevated clergy have held "Raves for Jesus" and introduced cardboard Clap-O-Meters into their churches so that, when Our Lord's name is mentioned, we applaud vigorously and the vicar moves the arrow round to the top category— "Pure Dead Brilliant!!" But the Church and State have made their feeble accommodations with pop culture mostly for reasons of self-doubt or strategy. Only Professor Gates & Co. have chosen to go over to the other side with such gusto—hipper than thou, cooler than thou, more pure dead brilliant than thou. It's not that pop stars want to be intellectuals, but that intellectuals want to be pop stars—a uniquely contemporary crisis. The threat to the European past comes not from mass vulgarization but from elite vulgarization. The most popular forms of contemporary culture—"Dr. Quinn, Medicine Woman," *The Bridges of Madison County*, Whitney Houston and Céline Dion ballads—are unchanged in their bourgeois sentimental efficiency from their equivalents a hundred years ago. What's different is that, whereas a century ago our betters were telling us to put down our parlor ballads for Mozart and Beethoven, now they tell us we should be listening to Rapeman or Suicide.

Conservatives are fond of quoting Cicero: "To know nothing of what happened before you were born is to remain ever a child." But what works as a put-down in Cicero's day isn't necessarily as effective in ours: one of the reasons we're not interested in anything that happened before we were born is precisely because we want to remain ever children. That would certainly appear to be the principle on which modern society operates. Mass culture is not democratic culture: it values certain groups over others. The music industry and motion pictures devote the bulk of their product to the young; TV advertisers prefer shows that attract a young demographic, presumably because those audiences are more susceptible to the unceasing swirl of pointless and interchangeable novelties on which a present-tense culture depends; last year, *The New York Times* reported with dismay that according to an NEA survey on the "graying" of arts audiences, the average age of theatergoers at five Broadway shows was 40.2 years. Given that American life expectancy is in the mid-seventies and that any four-year-old kid who wants to spend his evenings at Sondheim musicals ought to be in therapy, I'd say that figure was about smack dab where it should be. In essence, the *Times* and the NEA are fretting that Americans are too elderly for their art forms' preferred image.

But it's also true that as big a factor in the dismal immaturity of contemporary culture is our swollen academe. America now confers annually almost five times the number of degrees it bestowed in 1950; its college population is twice the size of its high school population; by 1993, to earn a bachelor's degree took on average 6.29 years. Yet President Clinton apparently won't be satisfied until *every* American goes to college. Possibly he has in mind the German model, which is rapidly approaching the point at which the average able-bodied male completes his education at thirty-nine, pursues the career for which he's been so thoroughly prepared for a couple of years and then takes early retirement at forty-two.

To what disciplines are these multitudes of elderly students submitting? None, naturally. Like so much of our arts and entertainments, the principal purpose is to defer adulthood. More college students means perhaps a teensy bit more Shakespeare but, sure as night follows day, or A.M. follows P.M., lots more Maya Angelou, more Rigoberta Menchu, more Afrocentrism, more Tarantino studies, women's studies, queer studies, transgender studies. . . . Certainly, multiculturalism doesn't extend to knowing the capital of Malaysia or the principal exports of South Africa. We have far more education at far greater cost than ever before, yet we are conspicuously less educated. If Bill Clinton seriously wishes to be remembered as the "education president," he might consider introducing a mandatory Federal school-leaving age of twelve.

In Vermont, the Supreme Court has just declared the state's funding of education unconstitutional on the grounds that one cannot have "equality of opportunity" if some towns are prepared to spend nine thousand dollars per pupil while others spend only six thousand. The system which sustained America's education for most of its history is, apparently, illegal. It seems self-evidently banal, given the money America's thrown at the public school system in recent years, to measure education by the size of the budget. A hundred years ago, we took a different view: the voters hired the teacher and boarded him out to the lowest bidder within the district; no hidden costs there. The trouble with Vermont's decision is that every movement toward statewide or Federal education systems is to the advantage of the teachers' unions and delivers the elementary schools further into the hands of the same people who've demolished the universities, people who seem determined to reduce the past to three or four ongoing grievance disputes. In some schools, they're already there. In San Francisco, you can't pray or sing hymns but every child gets to help make the banner for the Gay Pride parade.

President Clinton's answer to the woes of education is the Internet: he's committed to wiring up every classroom, whether it wants to be or not. Heaven knows why. Children don't exactly need to be encouraged to switch on their computers and other electronic toys, so it would be heartening to think that, for at least a few hours a day, they might be cajoled into opening a book. Besides, Mr. Clinton's optimism flies in the face of even recent history. Radio was supposed to be an educational tool: it started in the early Twenties with serious talks and live drama from the

Provincetown Players and "The American School of the Air"; today, it's a jukebox. TV was supposed to be an educational tool: it began with Leonard Bernstein explaining symphonic construction in prime time; today, it's a freakshow. Who seriously doubts that the Internet will follow the same trajectory? Pubescent boys, up in their rooms downloading Teri Hatcher all night, have already got the measure of the thing.

As that last kindergarten class trooped out of our academy building, many of them descendants of its very first class a century and a half earlier, it was hard not to feel that this next generation is the biggest experiment of all, caught between an omnipresent commercial culture which despises the past and an intellectual establishment which seeks to annex it for its own purposes. We should cherish those small-town Memorial Day and Fourth of July celebrations where nervous third graders in stovepipe hats and false beards recite the Gettysburg Address. Unlike our president, they can still be bothered to check. The past? It's history.

April 1997

The Postmodern Assault

Hilton Kramer

But the new barbarian is no uncouth
Desert-dweller; he does not emerge
From fir forests; factories bred him;
Corporate companies, college towns
Mothered his mind, and many journals
Backed his beliefs. He was born here.
—W. H. Auden, *The Age of Anxiety*

It is still deemed civilized to believe in European civilization.
—Matthew Craske, *Art in Europe 1700–1830*

I N THE issue of the London *Times Literary Supplement* for
March 6, 1996, readers of that venerable journal were
given a remarkable account of the kind of intellectual li-
cense which is now commonplace for scholars in high
places to impose upon objects of art-historical study. For
those who had not yet fully awakened to the implications
of the postmodern assault on the history and criticism of
the fine arts, it must have come as a rude shock to discover
just how far this bizarre mode of discourse had advanced in
its task of deconstructing the great artistic achievements of
the European past. For anyone who was already alert to the
depredations of the postmodernist juggernaut, this review

in the *TLS* was yet another melancholy reminder of how much ground has been lost to its malign imperatives.

The occasion was the publication by the Yale University Press of a book called *The Making of Rubens*. The author of this work—Svetlana Alpers—is a professor of the history of art at the University of California, Berkeley, and an influential eminence in her scholarly discipline. Among her earlier publications are books on Rembrandt and seventeenth-century Dutch still-life painting that were widely noticed and highly praised in both scholarly journals and the mainstream press. The reviewer for the *TLS* was Christopher Brown, curator of European painting at the National Gallery of Art in London and himself a distinguished scholar and connoisseur of the art that is the focus of Professor Alpers's study.

So troubled was Mr. Brown by the thesis propounded in *The Making of Rubens*, the title of which encompasses the kind of obscene pun that has become a hallmark of postmodernist criticism, that he felt obliged to apprise readers of the *TLS* of some background information on the scholarly debate that had preceded the publication of the book. It is thus necessary to quote at length from Mr. Brown's review not only for the exact character of Professor Alpers's project in *The Making of Rubens* to be clearly understood but for its significance as an example of the larger phenomenon it represents to be accurately assessed:

> At a plenary session of the conference of Historians of Netherlandish Art held in Boston in 1993, Svetlana Alpers discussed Rubens's treatment of the subject of Silenus, the corpulent, drunken follower of Bacchus, Falstaff to Bacchus's Prince Hal. It was interesting, she told us, that Rubens had painted and drawn this subject so often, and

even more interesting that he had represented this depraved figure in a relatively positive light. So far, so good. She then drew our attention to the fact that close behind Silenus, in Rubens's painting of the subject in Munich, was a smiling black man who pinches a fold of the flesh of Silenus's left leg. The purpose of this handhold, she continued, was to enable him to penetrate Silenus. While the audience was trying to come to terms with this metaphor, Alpers made it clear by forceful repetition that it was not a metaphor and that she was telling us that Rubens was here representing an act of homosexual anal sex. She then went on to describe Silenus as a self-portrait of Rubens, although his features bear not the remotest resemblance to those of the artist, well known from more conventional self-portraits. It is a self-portrait in the same sense, we are told, that Degas's "Woman Looking through Opera-Glasses" is a self-portrait.

In the silence that followed the lecture, the other plenary speaker, Elizabeth McGrath, with ironical understatement, voiced the doubt that "anything untoward" was going on in the picture. During the subsequent discussion, there was amazement that anyone who knew about the historical personality of Rubens and about ideas of decorum in seventeenth-century painting could seriously propose such an interpretation. Alpers's "buggery of Silenus" lecture has now been published with two others in a short, well-illustrated book with the deliberately ambiguous title *The Making of Rubens*. It is not, I think, unfair to characterize the lecture in this way because, although there is much else in it, Alpers is aware of the sensational nature of her interpretation. She has toned it down a little for publication. When we first encounter this idea, the black man "follows so close as to appear to be penetrating the huge body from behind." Later, any doubts that this is what is happening are abandoned.

One of the ideas at issue in this bizarre reading of Rubens's *Drunken Silenus* is, of course, the postmodern notion of "intentionality," which now beckons scholars in many humanistic disciplines to substitute for the verifiable data of historical research politically determined scenarios of their own invention—in other words, historical fictions. In this endeavor, which is designed to deconstruct the historical past for the purpose of bringing it into ideological alignment with the imperatives of postmodern discourse, a concentrated interest in perverse sexuality is a common priority. It derives its intellectual sanction from the new pseudo-disciplines of gender studies, gay and lesbian studies, and the even more comprehensive field of cultural studies, all of which have had the effect of transforming history into a mythology that at times bears a remarkable resemblance to Krafft-Ebing's *Psychopathia Sexualis*.

About the use which Professor Alpers makes of this slippery notion of "intentionality" in *The Making of Rubens*, Mr. Brown had this to say:

> She writes of the "intentionality of the painting," suggesting that this is in some way different from the intentionality of the artist. It raises the key point which applies to many of the ideas put forward in this book. What, precisely, is their status? In the case of Silenus, is Alpers telling us that Rubens deliberately threw aside all rules of seventeenth-century decorum? (In a long footnote, she admits to being unable to find any comparable scene in seventeenth-century art.) Does she believe that Rubens subcon-

sciously painted this shocking subject within contemporary conventions and so revealed the feminine aspect of his
art for which she argues? Or does she mean this to be a
subjective twentieth-century interpretation? At no point is
this issue clarified.

It can't be clarified, alas, because it is not in the nature of
postmodern discourse to acknowledge the validity of the
kind of distinctions—between, say, a subjective twentieth-
century interpretation and an objective seventeenth-century
cultural reality—that Mr. Brown was concerned to make in
this passage. The only "intentionality" that counts in *The
Making of Rubens* is that which Professor Alpers brings to
her critical project. What may be known or reasonably in-
ferred about Rubens's intentions in the matter are rendered
irrelevant to the inquiry.

Mr. Brown nonetheless persevered in offering the readers of the *TLS* a more conventional reading of Rubens—
based, as he wrote, on "the context of [the artist's] profound understanding of the Antique and his recreation of
numerous classical scenes":

> A more plausible explanation for what the black man is ac-
> tually doing is that he is pinching Silenus's flesh to show to
> the amusement of his companions that Silenus is so drunk
> that he no longer has any feeling in his leg.

For an art historian of Professor Alper's persuasion, however, such an unproblematic depiction of a satyr incapac-
itated by drunkenness would hardly qualify as a subject
worthy of serious attention. What would there be to deconstruct if the subject of the *Drunken Silenus* really was

taken to be a drunken Silenus? In the lexicon of post-modernist causes, alcohol abuse—unlike buggery, for example—has never enjoyed much of a priority. It just isn't sufficiently sexy in itself, and lavishing scrutiny on excessive insobriety would in any case risk being seen to support conventional bourgeois morality, which it is also the purpose of postmodernism to deconstruct. So the subject of the *Drunken Silenus* had to be reinvented to qualify as a suitably sexy object of postmodernist hermeneutics.

It had to be reinvented, moreover, for a mode of critical discourse that is devoid of aesthetic analysis. For what also needs to be taken into account in this postmodernist assault on the history and criticism of the fine arts is the absence of any newly formulated aesthetic judgments in determining the objects of critical scrutiny. The rejection of aesthetics—and of the connoisseurship that derives from the comparative aesthetic analysis of works of art—is indeed fundamental to the postmodern discourse about art.

Postmodern criticism is thus condemned to live, for the most part, off the inherited aesthetic and historical judgments of the very past it seeks to unmask and subvert. By the nature of its essentially political project, it is itself incapable of contributing any new aesthetic intelligence to our understanding of the art of the past. It cannot tell us why Rubens's painting *as a painting* is still worth our attention more than three centuries after its creation. It takes Rubens's importance for granted—granted, that is, by critical precedent—as it exploits his traditional position in the history of art in order to offer us instruction in subjects more congenial to the postmodern agenda. In the case of *The Making of Rubens*, the real subject turns out to be—what else?—"male femininity," which Rubens's depiction of

Silenus is alleged to represent. What for 157 pages has been masquerading as art history is actually a postmodern homily on the variety of human sexuality. Professor Alpers gives the whole game away in the closing paragraph of her book:

> When there is a rush, as there is today, to recognize and name the subversive, transgressive and the marginal, it is useful to be reminded that complex notions of identity and of identification are not new. It might be that what is now being construed as exceptional is instead fundamental to human nature and to the ways in which it is understood. Rubens's Silenus gives evidence of this as he confronts the condition of human generation and creativity. But, I must admit, Silenus was a marginal figure.

Unfortunately for anyone concerned about the future of the European past as far as the writing of art history is concerned, Professor Alpers's intellectual enterprise in *The Making of Rubens* is anything but marginal. It is, on the contrary, entirely representative of the intellectual catastrophe that has overtaken the writing of art history and art criticism in this last decade of the twentieth century, not only at the higher altitudes of academic specialization and prestige but in the popularization of postmodern discourse that has now insinuated itself into the college classroom, the art museums, and the mainstream critical press.

What a radical coterie of elite academics has been cooking up in learned journals and professional conferences for more than a generation is now being served, cafeteria-style, to masses of unwary students and museumgoers as reliable guides to the experience of art. Out of the postmodern seminars in the universities have come the new cadres of museum curators, who now embark upon their professional duties without the slightest knowledge of the kind of connoisseurship that was formerly the hallmark of their vocation, and they in turn further propagate the post-modern gospel—which is often the only thing they know about art—in the exhibition catalogues and wall texts that now compete for the public's attention with the art objects on display. For the postmodern assault is nothing if not fiercely didactic in its ideological mission—didactic, that is, about everything but the aesthetic distinctions that separate a work of fine art from the other objects of material culture that our civilization has produced in such profusion.

What this is likely to mean for the future of our under-standing of Europe's artistic past can be gleaned in this recent announcement from the Oxford University Press:

> Although art scholarship has undergone a radical change in recent years, this new thinking cannot be found in art book series now on the market. Moving away from the elitist, connoisseurial approach of the past, the *Oxford History of Art* seeks to clarify and illuminate its subjects by considering art (as well as architecture, photography, and design) in its social and cultural context. Series authors explore the aesthetic merits of a work and seek to answer such questions as: Why was the work created? What was it used for? What did contemporary critics and ordinary people think of it? And while the authors cover all the major artists and iconic masterpieces of art history, they also broaden the scope of their inquiries to include discus-sions of unfamiliar works often dismissed by traditional surveys and texts. Volumes on neglected subject areas such as Art and Sexuality, Art and Film, Women in Art, Native North American Art, and Melanesian Art will also be in-cluded in the series.

The first five volumes in this new *Oxford History of Art* have now been published, and by the year 2001 a total of some sixty titles is expected to complete the project. The result aspires to provide us with "a comprehensive, accessible library covering all aspects of art and architecture, East and West, from ancient civilizations to Cindy Sherman."

If the art of Europe continues, perforce, to loom very large in Oxford's new postmodern multiculturalist *History of Art*, that carefully chosen reference to the art of the American feminist photographer Cindy Sherman as the terminal achievement to be considered in this comprehensive chronicle of the world's art puts us on notice that the European past will not otherwise be "privileged," as they say, in this series. Indeed, to judge by the first two volumes to be devoted to European art in the new *Oxford History—Art and Society in Italy 1350–1500* by Evelyn Welch and *Art in Europe 1700–1830* by Matthew Craske—the specifically *artistic* achievements of the European past can scarcely be said to come up for consideration. The real focus of inquiry in these histories is on social, sexual, economic, and political developments, which works of art are merely cited as illustrating but are not discussed within the disciplines of their own creation.

Thus, despite the promise that "the aesthetic merits of a work" would be explored in the series, the new *Oxford History* is art history purged of all aesthetic analysis. It is art history as the socio-political history of material culture—art history, that is to say, as fodder for postmodernist deconstruction on a vast scale. It is art history with the mind of the artist left out.

Nor do the first two volumes on European art even pretend to explain to newcomers to their subjects—the readers primarily targeted by the series—why some artists have come to be considered "major" and certain works of art have over time acquired the status of "iconic masterpieces of art history." There are illustrations of certain works by Fra Angelico reproduced in *Art and Society in Italy 1350–1500*, for example, and some illustrations of Chardin reproduced in *Art in Europe 1700–1830*, but no discussion of the art of painting in either case.

As for what *is* discussed in these volumes that are being sold to us as *art* history, here is a representative excerpt from the section on "Art and the Household" in Evelyn Welch's *Art and Society in Italy 1350–1500*:

> The phrase used by the Florentine officials, that women were like "little sacks," was based on their understanding of human biology, one which was quite confused in this period. There were a number of competing theories of human conception and female anatomy on offer in the fifteenth century. The most widely accepted version was based on Aristotle's writings. According to this philosophical system all living creatures were composed of two basic binary opposites: they were either hot or cold, or wet or dry. Men were generally hot and dry; women were normally cold and wet. A human being was created by mixing the hot, active male seed with the cold, passive female menstrual fluid. This contact acted like rennet on milk, coagulating the fluid and initiating the development of a cheese-like foetus which gradually solidified. If there was enough heat available, the more perfect form, a male child would result; too much cold and damp resulted in a less perfect form, the female or "incomplete male."

This may not be as inventive as Professor Alpers's scenario

for *Drunken Silenus*, but it is equally useless as a means of comprehending some of the greatest achievements of European art.

But then, from a postmodern perspective, it may no longer be possible to speak of "European art," or even of "Europe." Or so, anyway, Matthew Craske hastens to warn us in the opening pages of *Art in Europe 1700–1830*. "If to ascribe to and perpetuate the model of 'European art' developing through grand and cogent phases can be held to be a matter of belief," he writes in the Introduction, "this book is declaredly the work of an infidel." The problem, as Mr. Craske understands it, is what he calls "a cosmopolitan vision of Europe," which is now said to be outdated. "Europe is assumed to be a distinct civilization which developed in cogent phases. This tendency reflects a tradition of cosmopolitan thought which . . . stretches back into the eighteenth century; a tradition of associating cultivation of mind, both in scholastic and connoisseurial fields, with the assumption of a cosmopolitan vision of European culture." Even worse, in his view, is that "it is still deemed civilized to believe in European civilization." Thus, while professing—or condescending—to write "in a spirit of respect for the faithful," Mr. Craske nonetheless acknowledges that in *Art in Europe 1700–1830* his "text gives priority to the discussion of the social and economic causes of art-historical change." The result is indeed art history with the mind— and the talent—of the artists left out.

In this wholesale critical deconstruction of the great artistic achievements of the European past the nihilist imperatives of contemporary art in the last two decades of the twentieth century are also, of course, directly implicated. It is from the perversities of postmodernist art, after all, that the revisionist historians have often taken their cues and

sanctions—not always openly acknowledged, to be sure—
in deconstructing the art of the past. This is especially true
in those cases where what Susan Sontag once called an
"erotics of art" is given—as it customarily is in postmodern
criticism—priority over standards of aesthetic judgment.

Without the radical revision of taste presupposed by the
acclaim lavished on the sexually bizarre photographs of
Robert Mapplethorpe by the contemporary art establishment, for example, it is unlikely that we should ever have
been treated to a spectacle like that of Professor Alpers's
"buggery of Silenus" lecture. In what Professor Alpers
called the "rush . . . to recognize and name the subversive,
transgressive and the marginal" in human sexuality, so as
to be duly understood and approved as "fundamental to
human nature," the art world's aggrandizement of the photographs Mapplethorpe devoted to "transgressive" sexuality
certainly played a considerable role. Mapplethorpe's achievement of eminence on the contemporary art scene had a lot
less to do with the aesthetic quality of his photography than
with its wayward sexual subjects, and the same is true, of
course, for the "buggery of Silenus" lecture.

For revisionist art historians determined to bring the past
into alignment with a postmodern agenda, Mapplethorpe
has indeed become something of a touchstone. The work is
just arty enough to pass for having some sort of claim on
aesthetic distinction, or "style," and the subject matter
serves as a guarantee of its required "transgressive" character. It is no doubt for reasons of this sort that a Mapplethorpe photograph was chosen to adorn the cover of
Graham Clarke's *The Photograph*, another of the initial titles
in the *Oxford History of Art* series, placing it firmly within
the framework of the postmodern scenario. In the book it-

self, Mapplethorpe's work is given closer attention than that of significantly greater photographers—Eugène Atget, for instance, and Walker Evans—for what one can only assume are the same reasons. It is certainly true that neither Atget's *oeuvre* nor Evans's would quite lend itself to the kind of analysis that Mr. Clarke is eager to devote to Mapplethorpe:

> Often Mapplethorpe . . . *dresses* for the camera—in a tuxedo, in leather, in make-up. Most contentiously, in a 1978 self-portrait he has inserted a bull-whip into his anus as he looks at the camera: an obviously radical and extrovert *reversal* of virtually all the conventions of the portrait photograph. These photographic portraits place themselves within a larger context of gender and identity, but *as* photographs they insist upon themselves as part of a continuing metamorphosis in which a single personality does not so much change as reject the codes through which identity, private as much as public, is assumed, determined, and declared.

We are thus dispatched once again to the gender studies seminar, where the mind of the postmodernist is securely anchored to sexual politics and the artistic issues in photography need not be pondered. Not surprisingly, in the chapter which Mr. Clarke devotes to "The Portrait in Photography," the subject he turns to immediately after Mapplethorpe is Cindy Sherman, of whose pictures he writes: "And just as Mapplethorpe explicitly questions heterosexual codes of being, so too does Sherman question the terms by which woman is to be known and viewed. . . . In the end there *is* no literal reality. All is construction and myth and, ultimately, self-enclosed fantasy." Which, come to think of it, is not an inaccurate way to sum up the quality of the whole postmodern agenda.

One of the questions that must inevitably be addressed about that agenda is whether in the end it really differs all that much from the modernism that preceded the current assault. Wasn't there, after all, a nihilist strain in modernism as well—and if so, in what ways may the postmodernist assault be distinguished from it?

Now it certainly has to be acknowledged that the nihilist imperative has been a discernible component—and often a deadly coefficient—of the modern movement for at least a hundred years; since, that is to say, the cry of *"Merde! Merde!"* was first heard in public in the debut performance of Alfred Jarry's *Ubu Roi* at the Théâtre de l'Oeuvre in Paris in 1896. That was the performance that prompted William Butler Yeats, who was in the audience, to make his famous prediction: "After us, the savage god." It was beyond even Yeats's clairvoyant powers, however, to imagine just how savage and perverse the gods of art would become a hundred years later, especially since Yeats's own art was always—whatever its other peculiaries—to stand at a great distance from "the savage god" he had glimpsed that fateful evening in Paris.

Between the cry of *"Merde! Merde!"* in *Ubu Roi* in 1896 and, say, "The Naked Shit Pictures," which the celebrated postmodernists Gilbert & George exhibited in London to enormous public acclaim in the 1990s, there is an obvious connection, to be sure, but some crucial differences as well, especially in the response accorded to these respective artistic endeavors by respectable opinion. Gilbert & George come to us in a line of descent that can be traced back to the Dadaist mystifications of Marcel Duchamp, who would not himself emerge as an artist-hero beloved by the academy and the art establishment until the early 1960s—until, that is, the advent of Pop Art and its most celebrated mascot, Andy Warhol. Prior to the 1960s, Duchamp was generally regarded as a minor figure in the modern movement —important for his role in the New York branch of Dada, to be sure, and a sideline player in the Surrealist movement later on, but a minor figure all the same. It was only in the 1960s, when Pop Art, Warholism, and the politics of the counterculture combined to give us our first glimpse of what would soon thereafter become the postmodern assault, that Duchamp was elevated to artistic sainthood— the subject of glossy-magazine profiles, museum retrospectives, academic studies, and intellectual hero worship—and the way was prepared for a takeover by his numerous progeny.

Some years ago, in an essay on "The Age of the Avant-Garde," I had occasion to suggest that the modern movement in the arts—which was what was meant by the avant-garde—was a far more complex cultural phenomenon than was commonly appreciated, that it harbored in fact an "agenda of internal conflict and debate, not only about aesthetic matters but about the social values that govern them":

> If the bourgeois ethos may be said to have both a "progressive" and a "reactionary" side, the avant-garde is similarly divided. At one extreme, there is indeed an intransigent radicalism that categorically refuses to acknowledge the contingent and rather fragile character of the cultural enterprise, a radicalism that cancels all debts to the past in the pursuit of a new vision, however limited and fragmen-

tary and circumscribed, and thus feels at liberty—in fact, compelled—to sweep anything and everything in the path of its own immediate goals, whatever the consequences. It is from this radical extreme, of which Dada, I suppose, is the quintessential expression, that our romance of the avant-garde is largely derived. But the history of the avant-garde is by no means confined to these partisans of wholesale revolt. It also boasts its champions of harmony and tradition. It is actually among the latter that we are likely to find the most solid and enduring achievements of the modern era. . . .

I further characterized the fundamental division of the modern movement as that "between art conceived as a form of guerrilla warfare and art conceived as a vital tradition."[1] What, then, did it mean for an earlier generation of avant-garde masters to see in their work a crucial link with such a tradition? Matisse spoke to this question in his "Observations on Painting" (1945), in which the principal subject is indeed the creative relation of young painters to the art of the past.

It is remarkable that Cézanne, like Gustave Moreau, spoke of the Masters of the Louvre. At the time he was painting his portrait of Vollard, Cézanne spent his afternoons drawing at the Louvre. In the evenings, on his way home, he would pass through the rue Laffitte, and say to Vollard: "I think that tomorrow's sitting will be a good one, for I'm pleased with what I did this afternoon in the Louvre." These visits to the Louvre helped him to detach himself from his morning's work, for the artist always needs such a

---

1 See the introductory essay in *The Age of the Avant-Garde* (1973).

break in order to judge and to be in control of his previous day's work.[2]

Today, however, modernism of this persuasion—the modernism that attached itself with so much conviction and intelligence (and genius!) to the vital traditions of European thought—is one of the principal targets of the postmodern assault, which derives its "tradition" from the guerrilla avant-garde's rejection of tradition.

It was also observed in "The Age of the Avant-Garde" that the dissensions generated by this division "tended to increase, both in ferocity and effect, more or less in direct ratio to the turbulence of the political scene." I was writing in the immediate aftermath of the counterculture of the 1960s, and what has happened in the long interim, of course, is that the ideology of that counterculture is now fully established as the governing spirit of mainstream cultural life. The guerrillas of the 1960s have become the cultural commissars of the 1990s. Whatever they have lost in the realm of electoral politics—and the effect of their cultural conquests does seem to have been a vast increase in the number of political conservatives who achieve election to public office—they have more than made up for in the "culture wars" that are now their principal arena of political action.

The postmodernist assault on tradition—moral tradition as well as the traditions of Western art and thought—is inevitably an assault on the European past, and with each passing year our cultural isolation from that past as anything more than a tourist attraction looks more and more

---

2 See Jack Flam's *Matisse on Art* (1995), p. 157.

irreversible. It isn't only in postmodern art histories like Matthew Craske's *Art in Europe 1700–1830* that a belief in "European civilization" is now under attack. Belligerent denunciations of "Eurocentric" educational programs in the service of a politically determined multicuturalist pedagogy are now commonplace and enjoy the sanction of governmental bodies and the even more influential taste-making powers of popular culture. In the realm of art history and the criticism of art, anyway, the ground to be retrieved is already immense.

May 1997

Experiments against Reality
Roger Kimball

I do not have much use for notions like "objective value" and "objective truth."
—Richard Rorty

The man who cannot believe his senses, and the man who cannot believe anything else, are both insane, but their insanity is proved not by any error in their argument, but by the manifest mistake of their whole lives.
—G. K. Chesterton

I N the foreword to his magnum opus, *European Literature and the Latin Middle Ages* (1948), the great German scholar Ernst Robert Curtius noted that his book, for all its daunting scholarship, was "not the product of purely scholarly interests." Rather, it

> grew out of a concern for the preservation of Western culture. It seeks to serve an understanding of the Western cultural tradition in so far as it is manifested in literature. It attempts to illuminate the unity of that tradition . . . by the application of new methods. . . . In the intellectual chaos of the present it has become necessary . . . to demonstrate that unity. But the demonstration can only be made from a

universal standpoint. Such a standpoint is afforded by La-
tinity.

It would not be easy to find a passage more at odds, in tone
or substance, with the sensibilities that dominate the cultural landscape today. Curtius's talk of "new methods"
might at first elicit some enthusiasm from trendy advocates
of literary theory: after all, the word "method" can be
counted on to affect them the way a ringing bell affected
Pavlov's dog. In fact, though, they would find Curtius's
patient investigation of literary *topoi*—for that was what he
meant by "new methods"—hopelessly *retardataire*. And
Curtius's method is the least of what sets him apart from
the reigning sensibilities. Much more important is his quiet
but determined concern for the "preservation of Western
culture," his effort to exhibit the "unity of that tradition,"
his faith in a "universal standpoint" from which the "intellectual chaos" of his time could be effectively addressed.
Even his turn to Latin, "the language of the educated
during the thirteen centuries which lie between Virgil and
Dante," marks him as an oddity in the present intellectual
climate.

Today, the very idea that there might be something dis-
tinctive about the Western cultural tradition—something,
moreover, eminently worth preserving—is under attack on
several fronts. Multiculturalists in the academy and other
cultural institutions—museums, foundations, the entertainment industry—busy themselves denouncing the West
as racist, sexist, imperialistic, and ethnocentric. The cultural
unity that Curtius celebrates is challenged by intellectual
segregationists eager to champion relativism and to attack
what they see as the "hegemony" of Eurocentrism in art,
literature, philosophy, politics, and even in science. The

ideal of a "universal standpoint" from which the achievements of the West may be understood and disseminated is derided by partisans of cultural studies and neo-pragmatism as parochial and, worse, dangerously "foundationalist."

Writing in the immediate aftermath of World War II, Curtius naturally had the assaults of totalitarianism chiefly in mind when he spoke of the "intellectual chaos" of his time. Today's cultural commissars do not—not yet, anyway—control any governments or police forces. But the intellectual and spiritual chaos they endorse is potentially as disruptive and paralyzing as any brand of nihilism. The political philosopher Hannah Arendt once described totalitarianism as an "experiment against reality." She had in mind, among other things, the peculiar mixture of gullibility and cynicism that totalitarian movements inspire, an amalgam that fosters an intellectual twilight in which people believe "everything and nothing, think that everything was possible and nothing was true." It is in this sense that the cultural relativists of today display a totalitarian cast of mind. Their efforts to disestablish the intellectual tradition of the West are so many experiments against reality: the reality of our cultural and spiritual legacy.

It is a simple matter to give examples and describe the effects of such experiments against reality. But uncovering their precise nature—what, finally, motivates them, what they portend—is more difficult. They are as amorphous as they are widespread and virulent. It is consequently easy to get lost in the maze of competing barbarisms: deconstruction, structuralism, postcolonialism, and queer theory for breakfast, postdeconstructive cultural studies and Lacanian feminism for lunch. Who can say what will be served up for dinner? The menu is endless, and endlessly hermetic. And yet there are recurrent themes, arguments, and attitudes.

Above all there are unifying suppositions, often only half-articulated, about the stability of human nature, the meaning of tradition, the scope and criteria of knowledge. In an appendix to his *Essays on European Literature*, Curtius again provides a striking counterexample to today's received wisdom when he speaks of the "essential connection between love and knowledge" and emphasizes the critic's *receptivity*, his subservience to the reality he seeks to understand. "Reception is the essential condition for perception," Curtius writes, "and this then leads to conception." At a time when the hubris of the critic is matched only by the fatuousness of his theories, Curtius's insistence that knowledge owes a perpetual debt to reality—that scholarship, as he puts it, "must always remain objective"—sounds a refreshingly discordant note.

In some ways, Curtius's reflections on the responsibilities of scholarship are—or would once have been—commonplace. The problem today is that such commonplaces have become uncommonly rare. The scholarly ideal of patient attentiveness is as démodé as a commitment to the ideal of objectivity. So it is that in these passing remarks Curitus touches on a matter of critical importance for anyone concerned with the future of the European past. Behind his insistence on the essentially receptive attitude of the critic is an acknowledgment that reality ultimately transcends our efforts to master it. It is reality that speaks to us, not we who lecture it. At the same time, Curtius's entire commitment to scholarship and "the preservation of Western culture" rests on a faith that the search for truth is not futile. If we must wait upon truth, we do not wait in vain. This twofold attitude—an acceptance of human limitation together with an affirmation of human capability—underlies his scholarly endeavor and links it to the great hu-

manistic tradition of which he is a late, eloquent spokesman. It is also, finally, what sets him at odds with the en-
emies of that tradition. There are two large questions at
issue in this conflict: the relation between truth and cultural
value, and the authority of tradition as the custodian of
mankind's spiritual aspirations.

Of the many things that have characterized the main current of European culture, perhaps none has been more
central than faith in the liberating power of truth. At least
since Plato described truth as the "food of the soul" and
linked it to the idea of the good, truth has had, in the West,
a normative as well as an intellectual component. In this
sense, knowing the truth has been held to be not only a
matter of comprehension but also of enlightenment, its at-
tainment a moral as well as a cognitive achievement. The
habit of judging "according to right reason," in Aristotle's
formula, was seen to be as much an expression of character
as intelligence. Saying yes to the truth involved ascent as
much as assent. Philosophy, the "love of wisdom," proposed freedom not simply from ignorance but also, cen-
trally, from illusion. "You shall know the truth," the Gospel
of St. John tells us, "and the truth shall set you free." The
optimism inherent in this imperative underlies not only the
mainsprings of Western religion but also the development
of its science and political institutions from the time of the
Greeks through the Enlightenment and beyond.

   Of course, this edifying picture has had plenty of competition. "What is truth?" asked Pontius Pilate as he washed
his hands, thus providing a role model for countless generations of cynics. At the end of *The Republic*, Socrates says
that the philosopher's "main concern" should be "to make a
reasoned choice between the better and the worse life, with

reference to the nature of the soul." But earlier in that dialogue he admits that many who devote themselves too single-mindedly to philosophy become cranks if not, indeed, *pamponērous*, "thoroughly depraved." The character of Thrasymachus, taunting Socrates with the declaration that "justice is nothing but the advantage of the stronger," provides an enduring image of the kind—or one of the kinds—of moral nihilist whose influence Plato feared.

In the modern age, no one has carried forward Thrasymachus's challenge more subtly or more radically than Friedrich Nietzsche. In a celebrated epigram, Nietzsche wrote that "we have art lest we perish from the truth." His disturbing thought was that art, with its fondness for illusion and make-believe, did not so much grace life as provide grateful distraction from life's horrors. But Nietzsche's real radicalism came in the way that he attempted to read life *against* truth. Inverting the Platonic-Christian doctrine that linked truth with the good and the beautiful, he declared truth to be "ugly." Suspecting that "the will to truth might be a concealed will to death," Nietzsche boldly demanded that "the value of truth must for once be experimentally *called into question.*" This is as it were the moral source of all those famous Nietzschean formulae about truth and knowledge—that "there are no facts, only interpretations," that "to tell the truth is simply to lie according to a fixed convention," etc. As Nietzsche recognized, his effort to provide a genealogy of truth led directly "back to the moral problem: *Why have morality at all* when life, nature, and history are 'not moral'?"

Nietzsche's influence on contemporary intellectual life can hardly be overstated. "I am dynamite," he declared shortly before sinking into irretrievable madness. He was right. In one way or another, his example is an indispensable background to almost every destructive intellectual movement this century has witnessed. The philosopher Richard Rorty summed up Nietzsche's importance when he enthusiastically observed that "it was Nietzsche who first explicitly suggested that we drop the whole idea of 'knowing the truth.'"

It can be argued that part of Nietzsche's influence has been due to misunderstanding. It was not entirely Nietzsche's fault, for example, that he became in effect the house philosopher for the Nazis. But it is not possible to exonerate Nietzsche entirely on that score, either. He would have been repelled by National Socialism, had he lived to see it, especially its anti-Semitism and *lumpen* elements. But his consistent glorification of violence, his doctrine of "the will to power," his distinction between "master" and "slave" morality, his image of the *Ubermensch* who is "beyond good and evil": they all played so neatly into the Nazis' hands because their brutality nicely answered to the brutality of the Nazis' requirements. Even if Nietzsche meant something different from what the Nazis meant, there was an element of like appealing to like when it came to their use of his ideas and rhetoric.

Nietzsche's intellectual and moral influence on our contemporaries betrays similar complexities. One imagines that Nietzsche would have loathed such poseurs as Jacques Derrida and Michel Foucault (to name only two). Such bad taste! Such bad writing! But their philosophies are inconceivable without Nietzsche's example. And, once again, there is a great deal in Nietzsche's thought that answers to the requirements of deconstruction, poststructuralism, and their many offshoots and permutations. Nietzsche's obsession with power once again is central, in particular his subjugation of truth to scenarios of power. (Foucault's insistence that truth is always a coefficient of "regimes of power" is simply Nietzsche done over in black leather.) And where would the deconstructionists be without Nietzsche's endlessly quoted declaration that truth is "a moveable host of metaphors, metonymies, and anthropomorphisms"? A deconstructionist without the word "metonymy" is a pitiful thing, like a dog missing its favorite bone.

Conceptually, such signature Nietzsche-isms as "everything praised as moral is identical in essence with everything immoral" add little to the message that Thrasymachus had for us twenty-five hundred years ago. They are the predictable product of nominalism and the desire to say something shocking, a perennial combination among the intellectually impatient. Nietzsche's real radicalism arises from the grandiosity of his hubris. His militant "God is dead" atheism had its corollary: the dream of absolute self-creation, of a new sort of human being strong enough to dispense with inherited morality and create, in Nietzsche's phrase, its "own new tables of what is good." This ambition is at the root of Nietzsche's goal of effecting a "transvaluation of all values." It is also what makes his philosophy such an efficient solvent of traditional moral thinking.

At least, that is the *substance* of what makes Nietzsche philosophical "dynamite." The detonator is supplied by Nietzsche's remarkable style. As a stylist Nietzsche had many faults. His rhetoric can be as grandiose as his megalomania. But almost everyone agrees that Nietzsche was an extraordinarily seductive, if sometimes hectoring, writer. And it must be said, too, that Nietzsche's rhetorical excesses were generally at the service of an abiding seriousness about deep issues. He may have been wrong about a great many things—about the most important things—but he was never frivolous. Unfortunately, many of Nietzsche's imitators and disciples have copied the extravagance of his manner while neglecting his ultimately serious purpose. Indeed, his example has done a great deal to enfranchise frivolity as an acceptable academic tic. When combined with the polysyllabic portentousness of Nietzsche's disciple Martin Heidegger—another major influence on the style of deconstruction—the effect is deadly: portentous frivolity, the worst of both worlds. Nietzsche once wrote that "one does not only wish to be understood when one writes, one wishes just as surely *not* to be understood." How he would have rued that sentence had he foreseen the rebarbative quality of the academic prose his writings helped to inspire!

One could easily fill a book with examples of the way that philosophy and the humanities generally have abandoned not only any commitment to clarity of expression but also the search for truth and, ultimately, faith in their own power as instruments of moral illumination. Such is the stuff of which glittering academic reputations are made today: humanists whose message is the end of humanism, philosophers bent on demonstrating the utter nullity of philosophy. Let us confine ourselves here to a couple of characteristic examples from one of Nietzsche's most influential heirs, the French deconstructionist Jacques Derrida. Inspired by Nietzsche, Derrida is always talking about philosophy as a "game" or a form of "play." So he begins his book *Dissemination* with this sentence: "This (therefore) will not have been a book." "Therefore," indeed. This is followed by a . . . no, not an explanation, but a sort of exfoliation, a luxuriance of verbal curlicues designed not to clear things up but to festoon the initial obscurity with cleverness. Such "games" pall quickly, of course, and so Derrida, like so many of his epigoni, tries to spice things up by injecting sex-talk wherever possible. He can't mention Rous-seau without dilating on masturbation, reflect on writing without bringing in incest, and so on. It's what D. H. Lawrence called sex in the head: an academic's frenetically anemic effort to demonstrate that, despite appearances to the contrary, there really is blood in his (or her) veins.

It can all be pretty distasteful, as anyone familiar with current scholarship in the humanities well knows. But the real obscenity is practiced upon language. Here is a rela-tively mild passage from the beginning of "Plato's Phar-macy," Derrida's famous essay on the *Phaedrus*:

> A text is not a text unless it hides from the first comer, from the first glance, the law of its composition and the rules of its game. A text remains, moreover, forever imper-ceptible. Its law and its rules are not, however, harbored in the inaccessibility of a secret; it is simply that they can never be booked, in the *present*, into anything that could rigorously be called a perception. . . . If reading and writ-ing are one, as is easily thought these days, if reading *is* writing, this oneness designates neither undifferentiated (con)fusion nor identity at perfect rest; the *is* that couples reading with writing must rip apart.
>
> One must then, in a single gesture, but doubled, read and write. And that person would have understood no-thing of the game who, at this, would feel himself author-ized merely to add on; that is, to add any old thing. . . . The reading or writing supplement must be rigorously prescribed, but by the necessities of a *game*, by the logic of *play*, signs to which the system of all textual powers must be accorded and attuned.

Perhaps this is the appropriate place to recall Chesterton's definition of madness as "using mental activity so as to reach mental helplessness." If one penetrates behind the skeins of Derrida's rhetoric, a moment's thought will show that the "rigorously prescribed" logic of his play is completely short-circuited by a simple fact: that reading is not, as it happens, the same thing as writing. Never was, never will be.

Such deliberate stupefaction—Derrida's proposition that writing is prior to speech provides another example—is at the heart of deconstruction. Derrida's most famous sentence is undoubtedly *il n'y a pas de hors-texte*, "there is nothing outside the text." This is short hand for denying that words can refer to a reality beyond words, for denying that truth has its measure in something beyond the web of our language games. It is, of course, a simple matter to *say* "There is nothing outside the text." It has a clever, radical sound to it. But is it true? If so, then there is at least one thing "outside" the text, namely the truth of the statement "There is nothing outside the text."

It is the same with all such pronouncements: "There is no such thing as literal meaning" (Stanley Fish), "All readings are misreadings" (Jonathan Culler), "Truth . . . cannot exist independently of the human mind" (Richard Rorty). Or, in slightly less staccato form, here is Fredric Jameson:

> The very problem of a relationship between thoughts and words betrays a metaphysics of "presence," and implies an illusion that universal substances exist, in which we come face to face once and for all with objects; that meanings exist, such that it ought to be possible to "decide" whether they are initially verbal or not; that there is such a thing as knowledge which one can acquire in some tangible and permanent way.

Not only are all these statements essentially self-refuting—does Stanley Fish literally mean "There is no such thing as literal meaning"?—but they also have the handicap of being continually refuted by experience. When Derrida leaves Plato's pharmacy and goes into a Parisian one, he depends mightily on the fact that there *is* an outside to language, that when he asks for *aspirine* he will not be given *arsenic* instead.

A great deal of Derrida's philosophy depends on the linguistic accident that the French verb *différer* means both "to differ" and "to defer." Out of this pedestrian fact he has spun a dizzying argument, the upshot of which is that the meaning of any text is perpetually put off, *deferred*. But, of course, if some unscrupulous pharmacist were to substitute arsenic for aspirin, Derrida would learn to reconnect the signifier with the signified right speedily, and he would lament, in the time that remained to him, his apostasy from the logocentric "nostalgia" for the "metaphysics of presence."

It is often pointed out that deconstruction and structuralism have become old hat, that the parade of academic fashion has passed on to other entertainments: cultural studies and various neo-Marxist hybrids of "theory" and the politics of grievance. This is partly true. It is certainly the case that the terms "deconstruction" and "structuralism" no longer have the cachet they possessed a decade ago. Nor does the name "Derrida" automatically produce the reverence and wonder among graduate students that it once did. ("Foucault," however, seems to have retained its talismanic charm.) There are basically two reasons for this. The first has to do with the late Paul de Man, the Belgium-born Yale professor of comparative literature, who in addition to being one of the most prominent practitioners of deconstruction, was—it was revealed in the late 1980s—an enthusiastic contributor to Nazi newspapers during World War II. That discovery, and above all the flood of obscurantist mendacity disgorged by the deconstructionist-structuralist brotherhood—not least by Derrida himself—to exonerate de Man, has cast a permanent shadow over deconstruction's status as a widely accepted instrument of intellectual liberation. The second reason is simply that, like any academic fashion, deconstruction's methods and vocabulary, once so novel and forbidding, have gradually become part of the common coin of academic discourse.

In fact, though, this very process of assimilation has assured the continuing influence of deconstruction and structuralism. The *terms* "deconstruction" and "structuralism" are not invoked as regularly today as they once were; but the fundamental ideas about language, truth, and morality that they express are more widespread than ever. Once at home mostly in philosophy and literature departments, their nihilistic tenets are cropping up further and further afield: in departments of history, sociology, political science, and architecture; in law schools and—God help us—business schools. Outside the academy, the rhetoric of deconstruction has penetrated into museums and other cultural institutions. Indeed, deconstructive themes and presuppositions have increasingly become part of the general intellectual atmosphere: absorbed to such an extent that, like the ideas of psychoanalysis, they float almost unnoticed, part of the ambient spiritual pollution of our time.

Although the language of deconstruction and structuralism is forbidding, the appeal of the doctrines is not hard to understand. It is basically a Nietzschean appeal. As the English philosopher and novelist Iris Murdoch observes in *Metaphysics as a Guide to Morals* (1992), "the new antimetaphysical metaphysic promises to unburden the intellectuals and set them free to play. Man has now 'come of age' and is strong enough to get rid of his past."

That, at least, is the idea—the promise issued but, like meaning in a deconstructionist's fantasy, always deferred. As Murdoch notes, part of what is objectionable in the deconstructivist-structuralist ethos "is the damage done to other modes of thinking and to literature." Dissolving everything in a sea of unanchored signifiers, deconstruction encourages us to blur fundamental distinctions: distinctions between intellectual disciplines, between fact and fiction, between right and wrong. Because there is "no such thing" as intrinsic value, there is at bottom no reason to respect the integrity of literature, philosophy, science, or any other intellectual pursuit. All become fodder for the deconstructionist's "play"—or perhaps "folly" would be a more appropriate term. The crucial thing that is lost is truth: the ideal, in Murdoch's words, of "language as truthful, where 'truthful' means faithful to, engaging intelligently and responsibly with, a reality which is beyond us."

With its doctrine of *il n'y a pas de hors-texte*, deconstruction is an evasion of reality. In this sense it may be described as a reactionary force: it hides from rather than engages with reality. But because deconstruction operates by subversion, its evasions are at the same time an attack: an attack on the cogency of language and the moral and intellectual claims that language has codified in tradition. The subversive element inherent in the deconstructive enterprise is another reason that it has exercised such a mesmerizing spell on intellectuals eager to demonstrate their radical *bona fides*. Because it attacks the intellectual foundations of the established order, deconstruction promises its adherents not only an emancipation from the responsibilities of truth but also the prospect of engaging in a species of radical activism. A blow against the legitimacy of language, they imagine, is at the same time a blow against the legitimacy of the tradition in which language lives and has meaning. They are not mistaken about this. For it is by undercutting the idea of truth that the decontructionist also undercuts the idea of value, including established social, moral, and political values. And it is here, as Murdoch points out, that "the deep affinity, the holding hands under the table, between structuralism and Marxism becomes intelligible." Most deconstructionists would seem to be unlikely revolutionaries; but their attack on the inherited values of our culture is as radical and potentially destabilizing as anything devised for Mr. Molotov.

The deconstructionist impulse comes in a variety of flavors, from bitter to cloying, and can be made to serve a wide range of philosophical outlooks. That is part of what makes it so dangerous. One of the most beguiling and influential American deconstructionists is Richard Rorty. Once upon a time, Rorty was a serious analytic philosopher. Since the late 1970s, however, he has increasingly busied himself explaining why philosophy must jettison its concern with outmoded things like truth and human nature. According to him, philosophy should turn itself into a form of literature or—as he sometimes puts it—"fantasizing." He is set on "blurring the literature-philosophy distinction and promoting the idea of a seamless, undifferentiated 'general text,'" in which, say, Aristotle's *Metaphysics*, a television program, and a French novel might coalesce into a fit object of hermeneutical scrutiny. Thus it is that Rorty believes that "the novel, the movie, and the TV program have, gradually but steadily, replaced the sermon and the treatise

as the principal vehicles of moral change and progress."
(One does not, incidentally, have to believe that sermons or
treatises were ever "the principal vehicles of moral change
and progress" to be convinced that novels, movies, and TV
programs are nothing of the sort now.)

As almost goes without saying, Rorty's attack on philosophy and his celebration of culture as an "undifferentiated
'general text'" have earned him many honors. In the early
1980s, he left his professorship at Princeton for an even
grander one at the University of Virginia; he is the recipient
of a MacArthur Foundation "genius" award; and he has
lately emerged as one of those "all-purpose intellectuals . . .
ready to offer a view on pretty much anything" that he ex-
tols in his book *Consequences of Pragmatism* (1982). Indeed,
Richard Rorty is widely regarded today as he regards himself: as a sort secular sage, dispensing exhortations on all
manner of subjects, as readily on the op-ed page of major
newspapers as between the covers of an academic book of
philosophical essays. The tone is always soothing, the
rhetoric impish, the message nihilistic but cheerful. It has
turned out to be an unbeatable recipe for success, patronizing the reader with the thought that there is nothing that
cannot be patronized.

In his essay about Derrida in *Contingency, Irony, Solidarity* (1989), Rorty wrote about the French philosopher in
glowing terms as someone who "simply drops theory" for
the sake of amoral "fantasizing" about his philosophical
predecessors, "playing with them, giving free rein to the
trains of association they produce." He himself strives to
follow this procedure. He does not, however, call himself a
deconstructionist. That might be too off-putting. Instead,
he calls himself a "pragmatist" or, more recently, a "liberal ironist." What he wants, as he explained in *Philosophy*

and the Mirror of Nature (1979), his first foray into post-philosophical waters, is "philosophy without epistemology," that is, philosophy without truth, and especially without Truth with a capital *T*.

In brief, Rorty wants a philosophy (if we can still call it that) which "aims at continuing the conversation rather than at discovering truth." He can manage to abide "truths" with a small *t* and in the plural: truths that we don't take too seriously and wouldn't dream of foisting upon others: truths, in other words, that are true merely by linguistic convention: truths, that is to say, that are not true. What he cannot bear—and cannot bear to have us bear—is the idea of Truth that is somehow more than that.

Rorty generally tries to maintain a chummy, easygoing persona. This is consistent with his role as a "liberal ironist," i.e., someone who thinks that "cruelty is the worst thing we can do" (the liberal part) but who, believing that moral values are utterly contingent, thinks that what counts as "cruelty" is a sociological or linguistic construct. (This is where the irony comes in: "I do not think," Rorty writes, "there are any plain moral facts out there . . . nor any neutral ground on which to stand and argue that either torture or kindness are [*sic*] preferable to the other.") Accordingly, one thing that is certain to earn Rorty's contempt is the spectacle of someone without sufficient contempt for the truth. "You can still find philosophy professors," he tells us witheringly, "who will solemnly tell you that they are seeking *the truth*, not just a story or a consensus but an honest-to-God, down-home, accurate representation of the way the world is." That's the problem with liberal ironists: they are ironical about everything except their own irony, and are serious about tolerating everything except seriousness.

As Rorty is quick to point out, the "bedrock metaphysical issue" here is whether we have any non-linguistic access to reality. Does language "go all the way down"? (Like Derrida, Rorty subscribes to the doctrine of *il n'y a pas de hors-texte*.) Or does language point to a reality beyond itself, a reality that exercises a legitimate claim on our attention and provides a measure and limit for our descriptions of the world? In other words, is truth something that we invent? Or something that we discover?

The main current of Western culture has overwhelmingly endorsed the latter view. For example, the "receptivity" that Curtius insisted upon for the critic is unintelligible without some such presupposition. But Rorty firmly endorses the idea that truth is merely a human invention. He wants us to drop "the notion of truth as correspondence with reality altogether" and realize that there is "no difference that makes a difference" between the statement "it works because it's true" and "it's true because it works." He tells us that "Sentences like . . . 'Truth is independent of the human mind' are simply platitudes used to inculcate . . . the common sense of the West." Of course, Rorty is right that such sentences "inculcate . . . the common sense of the West." He is even right that they are "platitudes." The statement "The sun rises in the east" is another such platitude. It is worth pointing out, however, that "the common sense of the West" has a lot to be said for it and that even platitudes can be true.

Rorty cavalierly tells us that he does "not have much use for notions like 'objective value' and 'objective truth.'" But then the list of things that Rorty does not have much use for is very long. For example, he wants us to get rid of the idea that "the self or the world has an intrinsic nature" because it is "a remnant of the idea that the world is a divine creation." Since for Rorty "socialization" (like language) "goes all the way down," he believes that there is no such thing as a self apart from the social roles it inhabits: "the word 'I' is as hollow as the word 'death.'" ("Death," he assures us, is an "empty" term.)

Rorty looks forward to a culture—he calls it a "liberal utopia"—in which the "Nietzschean metaphors" of self-creation are finally "literalized," i.e., made real. For philosophers, or people who used to be philosophers, this would mean a culture that "took for granted that philosophical problems are as temporary as poetic problems, that there are no problems which bind the generations together in a single natural kind called 'humanity.'" ("Humanity" is another one of those notions that Rorty cannot think about without scare quotes.)

Rorty recognizes that most people ("most nonintellectuals") are not yet liberal ironists. Many people still believe that there is such a thing as truth independent of their thoughts. Some even continue to entertain the idea that their identity is more than a distillate of biological and sociological accidents. Rorty knows this. Whether he also knows that his own position as a liberal ironist crucially depends on most people being *non*-ironists is another question. One suspects not. In any event, he is clearly impatient with what he refers to as "a particular historically conditioned and possibly transient" view of the world, i.e., the pre-ironical view for which things like truth and morality still matter. Rorty, in short, is a connoisseur of contempt. He could hardly be more explicit about this. He tells us in the friendliest possible way that he wants us to "get to the point where we no longer worship *anything*, where we treat *nothing* as a quasi divinity, where we treat

Roger Kimball

everything—our language, our conscience, our community —as a product of time and chance." What Rorty wants is philosophy without philosophy. The "liberal utopia" he envisions is a utopia in which philosophy as traditionally conceived has conveniently emasculated itself, abandoned the search for truth, and lives on as a repository of more or less bracing exercises in fantasy.

In his book *Overcoming Law* (1995), the jurist and legal philosopher Richard Posner criticizes Rorty for his "deficient sense of fact" and "his belief in the plasticity of human nature," noting that both are "typical of modern philosophy." They are typical, anyway, of certain influential strains of modern philosophy. And it is in the union of these two things—a deficient sense of fact and a belief in the unbounded plasticity of human nature—that Nietzsche's legacy bears its most poisonous fruit. When Rorty, expatiating on the delights of his liberal utopia, says that "a postmetaphysical culture seems to me no more impossible than a postreligious one, and equally desirable," he perhaps speaks truer than he purposed. For despite the tenacity of nonirony in many sections of society, there is much in our culture—the culture of Europe writ large—that shows the disastrous effects of Nietzsche's dream of a postmetaphysical, ironized society of putative self-creators. And of course to say that such a society would be as desirable as a postreligious society amounts to saying also that it would be just as *un*desirable.

Like his fellow liberal ironists, Rorty takes radical secularism as an unarguable good. For him, religion, like truth—like anything that transcends our contingent self-creations—belongs to the childhood of mankind. Ironists are beyond all that, and liberal ironists are beyond it with a smile and a little joke. But of course whether our culture really is "postreligious" remains very much an open question. That liberal ironists such as Richard Rorty make do without religion does not tell us very much about the matter. In an essay called "The Self-Poisoning of the Open Society," the Polish philosopher Leszek Kolakowski observes that the idea that there are no fundamental disputes about moral and spiritual values is "an intellectualist self-delusion, a half-conscious inclination by Western academics to treat the values they acquired from their liberal education as something natural, innate, corresponding to the normal disposition of human nature." Since liberal ironists like Richard Rorty do not believe that anything is natural or innate, Kolakowski's observation has to be slightly modified to fit him. But his general point remains, namely that "the net result of education freed of authority, tradition, and dogma is moral nihilism." Kolakowski readily admits that the belief in a unique core of personality "is not a scientifically provable truth." But he argues that, "without this belief, the notion of personal dignity and of human rights is an arbitrary concoction, suspended in the void, indefensible, easy to be dismissed," and hence prey to totalitarian doctrines and other deformations.

The Promethean dreams of writers such as Derrida and Rorty depend critically on their denying the reality of anything that transcends the prerogatives of their efforts at self-creation. Traditionally, the recognition of such realities has been linked with a recognition of the sacred. It is a mistake typical of intellectuals to believe that this link can be severed with impunity. This, too, is something that Kolakowski sees clearly. As he argues in another essay, "The Revenge of the Sacred in Secular Culture," "culture, when it loses its sacred sense, loses all sense." He continues:

With the disappearance of the sacred, which imposed limits to the perfection that could be attained by the profane, arises one of the most dangerous illusions of our civilization—the illusion that there are no limits to the changes that human life can undergo, that society is "in principle" an endlessly flexible thing, and that to deny this flexibility and this perfectibility is to deny man's total autonomy and thus to deny man himself.

It is a curious irony that self-creators from Nietzsche through Derrida and Richard Rorty are reluctant children of the Enlightenment. In his essay "What is Enlightenment?," Immanuel Kant observed that the Enlightenment's motto was *sapere aude*, "Dare to know!" For the deconstructionist, the liberal ironist, and other paragons of disillusionment, that motto has been revised to read "Dare to believe that there is nothing to know." The Enlightenment sought to emancipate man by liberating reason and battling against superstition. It has turned out, however, that when reason is liberated entirely from tradition—which means also when it is liberated entirely from any acknowledgment of what transcends it—reason grows rancorous and hubristic: it becomes, in short, something irrational.

It is in this sense that anyone concerned with the future of the European past must approach the Enlightenment and its legacy with conflicted feelings: in a spirit that is as ready to criticize as to endorse. To be sure, few of us would wish to do without the benefits of the Enlightenment. As the sociologist Edward Shils pointed out in his 1981 book *Tradition*, the Enlightenment's "tradition of emancipation from traditions is . . . among the precious achievements of our civilization. It has made citizens out of slaves and serfs. It has opened the imagination and the reason of human beings." Nevertheless—as Shils also understood—to the extent that Enlightenment rationalism turns against the tradition that gave rise to it, it degenerates into a force destructive of culture and the manifold directives that culture has bequeathed us. Like so many other promises of emancipation, it has contained the seeds of new forms of bondage. Philosophy has been an important casualty of this development. It is no accident that so much modern philosophy has been committed to bringing us the gospel of the end of philosophy. Once it abandons its vocation as the love of wisdom, philosophy inevitably becomes the gravedigger of its highest ambitions, interring itself with tools originally forged to perpetuate its service to truth.

Reflecting on the ambiguous legacy of the Enlightenment, especially the accelerating campaign against traditional sources of moral and intellectual direction, Shils went on to warn that "the destruction or discrediting of these cognitive, moral, metaphysical, and technical charts is a step into chaos. Destructive criticism which is an extension of reasoned criticism, aggravated by hatred, annuls the benefits of reason and restrained emancipation." Today, the effects of that annulment are evident everywhere. At stake is not simply the future of an academic discipline but the deepest sources of our moral and intellectual self-understanding. In *Philosophical Investigations*, Wittgenstein rightly remarked that "all philosophical problems have the form 'I have lost my way.'" At a moment when so much of intellectual life has degenerated into an experiment against reality, perhaps our primary task is facing up to the fact that many of the liberations we crave have served chiefly to compound the depth of our loss.

June 1997

Contributors

ANNE APPLEBAUM writes a weekly political column for the London *Evening Standard* and contributes to *Foreign Affairs*, *The Wall Street Journal*, and *The Washington Post*. She is the author of *Between East and West: Across the Borderlands of Europe*, on nationalism and the former Soviet bloc.

JOHN GROSS, former editor of *The Times Literary Supplement*, is the theater critic for the London *Sunday Telegraph*. He is the author of *The Rise and Fall of the Man of Letters* and *Shylock*, and the editor of several anthologies, including *The Oxford Book of Comic Verse* and *The Oxford Book of Essays*.

JOHN HERINGTON, until his death this year, was Talcott Professor of Greek Emeritus at Yale University. His books include translations of *Prometheus Bound* (with James Scully) and *The Persians* (with Janet Lembke), as well as *Aeschylus* and *Poetry into Drama: Early Tragedy and the Greek Poetic Tradition*.

ROGER KIMBALL is the managing editor of *The New Criterion* and the author of *Tenured Radicals: How Politics Has Corrupted Our Higher Education*. He is a frequent contributor to *The Wall Street Journal*, the London *Spectator*, and other magazines. He is currently writing a book about America's cultural revolution.

CONTRIBUTORS

HILTON KRAMER is the editor of *The New Criterion* and the author of *The Age of the Avant-Garde* and *The Revenge of the Philistines*. He is the art critic of *The New York Observer* and writes the weekly "Media Watch" column for the *New York Post*. His latest book, *Abstract Art: A Cultural History*, is forthcoming.

DAVID PRYCE-JONES is the author of nine novels as well as many works of nonfiction, including *The Strange Death of the Soviet Empire*, *Paris in the Third Reich: A History of the German Occupation, 1940–1944*, and *The Closed Circle: An Interpretation of the Arabs*.

FERDINAND MOUNT has been the editor of *The Times Literary Supplement* since 1991. His most recent novel is *The Liquidator*. Other books include *The Subversive Family* and *The British Constitution Now*. He was head of the Prime Minister's Policy Unit under Margaret Thatcher from 1982 to 1984. He currently writes a column for the *Sunday Times*.

ROGER SCRUTON is the editor of *The Salisbury Review*. His books include *Art and Imagination*, *The Meaning of Conservatism*, *The Aesthetics of Architecture*, and *Modern Philosophy: An Introduction and Survey*. His latest book, *The Aesthetics of Music*, is forthcoming from Oxford University Press.

MARK STEYN writes for the London *Daily Telegraph* and the *Sunday Telegraph*. He is the theater critic of *The New Criterion* and the film critic of the London *Spectator*. His column "Culture Vultures" appears regularly in *The American Spectator*.

KEITH WINDSCHUTTLE is the author most recently of *The Killing of History: How Literary Critics and Social Theorists Are Murdering Our Past*, forthcoming from The Free Press. He is the publisher of Macleay Press, Sydney.

Acknowledgments

The editors would like to take this opportunity to acknowledge the dedicated help of our colleagues Francesca Marx, Robert Richman, and David Yezzi, whose unstinting efforts helped make this book a reality.

It gives us great pleasure also to acknowledge the many individuals and institutions whose committed support for *The New Criterion* over the years has made our endeavors possible. We wish to thank in particular the Lynde and Harry Bradley Foundation, the John M. Olin Foundation, and the Sarah Scaife Foundation, without whose stalwart support *The New Criterion* would not exist.

We are especially grateful for the special grants from the Rosenkranz Foundation and the Lynde and Harry Bradley Foundation that have supported our series on the future of the European past and its publication in book form.

Index

223

INDEX

Ohlendorf, Otto, 22, 23
Oleksy, Jozef, 43
Ondaatje, Michael, *The English Patient*, 101
Orange Prize, 17
Ortega y Gasset, José, 5, 90
Orwell, George, 9
Ottoman empire, 129
Oxford History of Art (book), 184–188
Oxford Illustrated History of Christianity (book), 147
Ovid, 115

Pal Joey (musical), 158
Palach, Jan, 32
Pasolini, Pier Paolo, 9
Pavarotti, Luciano, 72
Penguin Books, 78
Pennac, Daniel, 14
Perseus Project, 114, 117
Perón, Juan and Eva, 129
Philip II, 133, 134
Picasso, Pablo, 7, 9
Plath, Sylvia, 83
Plato, 117, 199; *Phaedrus*, 204; *The Republic*, 199–200
Plumb, J(ohn) H(arold), *The Death of the Past*, 90, 97
Plutarch, 115
Poland, 14, 31–33, 35, 40, 43–44, 48; lustration in, 36–37
Pop Art, 191
Popper, Karl, 9
Porter, Cole, 64
Posner, Richard, *Overcoming Law*, 214
Postmodernism, 13, 177–194

passim; in art, 177, 180; in history, 138; in music, 68
Presley, Elvis, 167
Proulx, E. Annie, *The Shipping News*, 101
Proust, Marcel, 96
Purcell, Henry, 58
Pétain, Henri, 7, 23

Rabelais, François, 96
Rabin, Yitzak, 83
Rainger, Ralph, "Love Is Just around the Corner," 167
Ranke, Leopold von, 139, 140, 145
Reich, Steve, 68
Reich-Ranitski, Marcel, 14
Rembrandt, 178
Remnick, David, *Lenin's Tomb*, 39
Renaissance, 51, 112; in England, 115
Reyes, Alina, 14
Richler, Mordecai, *Solomon Gursky Was Here*, 101
Robin Hood, 81
Robin, Leo, "Love Is Just around the Corner," 167–168
Rodgers, Richard, 64
Rodman, Dennis, 162
Rolin, Dominique, 14
Rolling Stones, The, 169
Romania, 44, 48
Roosevelt, Franklin, 29, 129
Rorty, Richard, 195, 201, 209–216; *Consequences of Pragmatism*, 210; *Contingency, Irony, Solidarity*, 210; *Philosophy and the Mirror of Nature*, 211
Rosenberg, Alfred, 22

231